Intermit. Explosive disorder

The Visionary Messenger

Adele Linsalata

© 2007 Adele Linsalata
All Rights Reserved.

No part of this publication may be reproduced, stored in a retrieval system, or transmitted, in any form or by any means, electronic, mechanical, photocopying, recording, or otherwise, without the written permission of the author.

First published by Dog Ear Publishing
4010 W. 86th Street, Ste H
Indianapolis, IN 46268
www.dogearpublishing.net

ISBN: 978-159858-501-8

This book is printed on acid-free paper.

Printed in the United States of America

Dedication

With all of my heart this book is lovingly dedicated to my husband Larry, and all my children; Ash, Sam, Thomi, Tyler and Brooke. May you always know I am and have always been truly Blessed to have all of you here with me in this lifetime. I hope you never lose your sense of wonder, may you never take one single breath for granted and when you get the choice to sit it out or dance I hope you dance

I hope you dance

In loving Memory to MOM - Joan M. Bellofatto

Acknowledgements;

As we all take a moment in time to look back to all those who have assisted and guided us in our lives to be all that we are here to be and to those who have been with me for so long as to love me during this time of writing from my heart and inner soul in my own responsibility for the words you are about to read, I also gratefully acknowledge the assistance and guidance from The Blessed Mother and Jeshua, my Counsel of One- The Angelic Wise Ones, all of my loved ones in the Spiritual Kingdom, Those in the Angelic Realms and Ascended Masters, Jane Niece- for finally opening the door one day to say Hello, Joanne Fort -for her loveliness and kindness going through these words, Sherry B. True- for always being there for me, Kate Large- our true Earth Angel. To Randy for making all of these pages possible as he was thrown into assisting me with completing this book. To each and everyone of my students, I love you all so much and thank you for your support and for taking the time to do your homework!

But, most of all I want to acknowledge my Mom and Dad, I love you so much.

You gave so much through thick and thin without even knowing how much you proved and showed to me that true Love will always keep us connected until the ends of time. For you have given so much to me in this life which I needed to Always Be Your Daughter!!!

Table of Contents

Introduction	Page 1
Chapter 1: My First Messenger	Page 5
Chapter 2: Lessons from the Old School	Page 26
Chapter3: Newbies and Sleepers	Page 43
Chapter 4: Society's Conditioning	Page 51
Chapter 5: The Visionary "Eyes Wide Open"	Page 57
Chapter 6: Psychometry	Page 62
Chapter 7: Truth Indicator	Page 65
Chapter 8: Death and Transitioning, How I See it	Page 69
Chapter 9: Understanding and Responsibility	Page 79
Chapter 10: Building your Foundation	Page 89
Chapter 11: The Miracles of Meditation	Page 102

Chapter 12: The Spiritual Realms of your
Guides and Teachers   Page 109

Chapter 13: Loved Ones in the Spiritual
Realms   Page 130

Chapter 14: Contracts   Page 138

Chapter 15: Religion and the Message   Page 143

Chapter 16: Cleansing and Clearing   Page 161

Chapter 17: Words to Leave You by   Page 174

Guided Meditation CD's   Page 179

Introduction

Do you understand the word on the streets right now is Spiritual Evolution? Nine out of ten people you know are having a spiritual awakening, yet most do not even realize it. They are in contact with spirit each day, but because of society's conditioning, they live right through it. They believe that their depression, anxiety and stress come from nothing more than dealing with money and family issues. But what they are really asking for on a deeper level deep within their being is an understanding of why they are going through it all in the first place. They go about their own day over and over again, trying to hold onto life without even considering all that life is.

The truth is that stress, anxiety and depression are prevalent in today's world because most people are trying to catch up with that which humankind believes will make them happier, healthier and more in control of their lives and those around them, only to fall into sickness or confusion when nothing plays out as their whole body has led them to believe. Actually, where their whole being is leading them is toward a remembrance of their spiritual self and their development in moving forward to what they have contracted to do in this physical lifetime. Their souls are calling so deep that no matter what they do, they cannot go far from it.

Perhaps you have been hearing that calling, perhaps assisted by your angels and guides. Maybe you are coming to understand that there is no evading that which you are here to be or do while living here on Mother Earth. You may be one who knows that we all have a divine mission and at this moment in time, and you are feeling beckoned to get started towards your own enlightenment, which is waiting for you. If so, I welcome you. I am a visionary messenger, which I define this way:

Visionary – seer, prophet, futurist, creative.

Messenger – courier, envoy, herald.

Knowing at this time that in this life I am a visionary messenger is a very peaceful, wonderful feeling. I love my life right now; it is the most magnificent thing in the world. I know as you read the pages of this book, you too will see how you are the most magnificent being right now, in this moment and for all that is to come. I hope and trust that you will resonate with what I share and that you know deep in your heart that you have come home. You have found another whom you can identify with, someone who is describing everything you feel and do. In these pages I give you peace and an understanding that you are not alone, crazy, weird or different. I remind you that you are free to do whatever your heart is calling you to do, whether that be as a medium, psychic, teacher or any kind of spiritual being in the world. To those of you who already know a little about spiritual development and want to know more because you sense that there is still something missing, you too will see similarities in your life right now that will help you to open the door of your own identity and understanding.

For as our hearts are the child-like innocence so will those be who enter the kingdom of thy father.

For a long time everyone has asked me to write a book, not just about what I do and who I am but about what we all do as spiritual lights in this physical world. A book, too, that would acknowledge my own journey of triumphs and heartache. So here is that book, and I hope you will find value in what you discover in it. I hope it will touch your heart and life, start you on your spiritual journey and help you know that you are truly not alone. You too can start to see why you are here on this planet we call earth, why you have decided to be here. You can begin to understand the lessons or victories you are here to discover and work through. I wish you all the Love from the Divine, and I know that you truly are the Divine, a reality that is so true that your heart will open to it as your journey begins.

So too does my heart open. And in the first chapter, I give to you my own account of the beginning of what has been a unique and marvelous Divine journey.

Chapter I

MY FIRST MESSENGER

I was born into a large family with six brothers, and now I have an extended family of sisters-in-law, nieces and nephews and of course my own children and husband. When it comes to patience and acceptance, these are the ones we look towards to give us all that we think we need in our validation with our work within the spiritual realms. We try to talk to them and help them understand that this is a wonderful gift a joyous reunion as a spiritual being. With the ability to help and serve so many, as hard as we try we end up secluding ourselves from those whom we love by that mistake, by rushing too soon.

Forty years ago, I was not rushing. I was sitting at my grandmother's kitchen table playing the nightly card game of rummy with my cousins, uncle and grandfather when I looked up to see a man standing at the back door. He was smiling and seemed happy and sad at the same time. He did not speak, but I could hear him say "hello." At first I just kept playing cards with everyone, but then I asked my uncle if the man at the back door could come in and sit down and play cards with us. Well, my cousins started laughing at me. "There's no one there," they insisted. I should stop it and just finish the game. When I kept trying to tell them about the man, they started with the bogeyman game in which I always came out the loser. If they did not see him and maybe if I switched seats, I would not see him either.

I went around the table and started playing cards again as I sat on my grandfather's lap. As the night went on, I finally turned my head and looked behind us and, sure enough, he was still standing there. He had soft nice brown eyes. Since I was now sitting closer, I could see him clearer and knew he looked familiar. Then I remembered, I remembered the trip we just went on, a trip far away, and I saw this man lying in a bed with lots of flowers around him. Everyone was sad, and I was told to go up to the man in the bed and give him a goodbye kiss. I remember it so well because when I went to kiss him goodbye he sat up and said, "You don't have to say goodbye. I am not going anywhere; I will be around when you need me." I started laughing, and then it was my brother's turn to kiss him goodbye. My brother started crying; he did not want to kiss him goodbye. He was afraid to do it. I just stood there beside my dad as my mom calmed my brother down, and I remember feeling so much sadness and heartache from my dad. I tried to let him feel that everything would be okay and that his daddy was not going anywhere. He was here with us, smiling, giving my dad a large hug. However, I was shuffled along out of the room away from my dad.

Now I remember: this man standing at the back door was the same one. He was my grandfather from New York, and he was here as he promised. When I tried to tell everyone that he was here standing at the door, they laughed and told me I was crazy, to stop talking like that, that it was not nice. At the time, I was staying with my grandparents, who had a large house that my cousins, aunt and uncle also lived in; they lived upstairs on the second level. My bedroom wall was right by the stairs leading to their rooms, and I could always hear them as they went up and down the steps. As I went to bed that night, I kept dreaming of my grandfather from New York and wondering how in the world he got get here. I also wondered if my dad knew his father was here. Where was my dad, anyway? Did his father not go by and say hello to him?

I woke up to the sun shining bright in my room, and I knew it was going to be a great day. I had lots to do helping my grandmother with the wallpaper in the next room, and she always let me sew some clothes for my dolls with the leftover fabric. As the day went on and I finished my sewing, I went outside to play. My grandmother had many cats around; they never came in the house but were content lying around outside. As I was going towards the walnut tree, there he was standing there as if he was waiting for me. He reached down, picked me up and gave me a big hug and kiss. Both of us then sat under the tree. I asked him how he got there, and where was my dad? Did he not go to see Dad? Did not Dad want to come see me too? Mom was going to be mad when she found out he did not stop by to see her. She really liked my grandfather; he was kind to her. He started laughing and said, "One question at a time." He did stop by and see my dad, and Dad was doing just fine. Yes, he said hello to Mom too. She was looking pretty as ever, but the boys were keeping her busy right now.

He let me know how he just wanted to come by to see me and introduce me to some of his old friends he had met up with and how they would be the best of friends with me too. I was so happy. Then he turned me around, and I saw the most beautiful person standing there. She was wearing a divine dress of pink that flowed all around her. She had long brown hair and large bright eyes. She introduced herself and said her name was Marie, and she was going to be my very best friend until the end of time. I felt so soft and so much love from my new friend Marie. Then we all sat down and started playing a game called I Spy.

Over the next several days, Grandfather brought many friends with him on his visits. He introduced each one to me, and then we would all sit down and play different games. We played school a lot. I loved to listen to all their stories. One of my favorites was about a lovely young woman who was destined to be a great princess. She would bring love, laughter and so much light to many. She would heal them and show them the way to fulfill their own destiny, and then they would all live on this beautiful planet where each of their heart's desires would be freely there for them. Each day that Grandfather and his friends came, I learned as much as I could for I truly wanted to be so much like this lovely young lady.

Then there were the little people. These were the ones who would glow different colors. There was a clearness about them, almost as if they were in see-through bubbles, and when I looked into their eyes I could see really far inside, wherever I wanted to see. They would fly all about, and I would run to catch up to them, spread my arms out and wish so hard I could be like them, to fly among the birds, to go so fast that no one could catch me. These little ones would teach me about the trees and plants in my grandmother's yard. They were not always nice and would sometimes push me in the weeds and laugh as I came out crying to my grandmother.

Then the lovely angels would come. They beamed in radiant, multicolored light, and they sang the most precious of songs as they watched over everyone in my family. They seemed to know who every one in my family was, even though my cousins and other family members never said hello to them. These three did not mind. They would say to me, "Sometimes the older ones have so much earth work to do. They do not seem to see the little ones or angels as you do. We still assist them; do not upset yourself so. It is not meant to be for them at this time."

I was told that the greatest visitor was arriving in the coming days. By now, I had my own group of friends who were always with me. My grandfather said these three ladies were very special, and they were going to keep teaching and playing with me. I was to listen to them, and they would listen to me even though they were adults. They would not get mad at me. They would not tell me to hush up but would listen to me and show me what I needed to understand.

As I was lying in bed that night, I started to hear footsteps going up and down the stairs next to my bed. I was confused. My aunt and uncle were not home as they had taken my cousins and had gone out for the night. The noise was getting louder, though, so I called out to my grandmother. She came in and said she did not hear any noise; no one else was home and I should hush up and go to sleep. She gave me a kiss, and I closed my eyes. There it was again! Someone was running up and down the stairs. I got out of bed, went over to the door and looked up the steps. Sure enough, standing at the top of the stairs where the two bedrooms faced each other were all these people trying to get past each other and go into my cousin's room. I yelled again for my grandmother. This time she came in and asked me, "What in the world is going on and why are you not in bed?" I started crying as I told her all about the people upstairs, and how I did not like them very much. My grandmother turned on the light and went upstairs. Then she came back down and put me to bed, telling me that no one was up there and to get to sleep and stop trying to scare myself. As she left the room, I laid there and could not understand what was going on. I did see those people; they were all in a hurry. Maybe they knew Grandma was coming and hid under all the beds or in the attic.

I finally feel asleep that night, and I remember waking up in the morning to find my grandfather from New York sitting on my bed. He asked me if I had sweet dreams. I told him yes and then about all the people rushing up the steps last night and how Grandma was upset with me. He just sat there smiling, and his eyes were all lit up. I felt so much warmth coming from him. He told me he believed me, and it was all right. He would go and look, and get rid of anyone who was upstairs. I was so happy that I gave him a big hug and went to go get breakfast. I did not see him until later that day. He was waiting once again out by the tree with Marie at his side. I set up a table, and we would have tea with sandwiches as we played school. They told me of a great lady who loved me very much and how I would be meeting her soon. She loved children and took great care of them when they called out to her. She was going to visit here under the tree and wanted to meet with me. I was to call her Mother; and yes, even though I already had a mother, this lady was a mother to her too.

Grandfather and Marie also told me about great things that would happen in the world. They told me how I was to look at what was going on, how to understand all of the information I was getting. How I could be able to see things that would be happening. How I was to try to understand what was going on and tell people about it so they could make it better How to see and listen to the little people in the grass and in nature. How no one was better than another and that I had a large family who would always be with me. They taught me about the people who needed to go home, as they did not have a home here anymore. They all had been in a bed just like Grandpa with flowers all around and those who were sad about them. But these people did not go where my grandfather went; they were still walking around and searching for home. They needed help, and they would want me to help them to get home. Well, I did not think I could do that. Grandma and Granddaddy would be very mad and upset if I walked around with all these people taking them to their homes. They both hugged me tight and said not to worry; no one would get mad. I did not have to go anywhere. The people would come here to me; I just had to see them and talk them into going home to the light. Well, I was not sure if I could, but if my grandfather said I could, I would help him and do it.

That night as I was sleeping, I remember waking up. A man who kept looking at me real funny was standing beside my bed. He did not seem nice, and he was very upset that I was sleeping. I asked him his name, and he said Timothy. They told him to come here. He did not know why; but well…. here he was, and just what did I think I was going to be able to do? Well, I did not know what to do with him, so I just started talking to him and asking him questions about his family. He did not like to talk at first, and he would get mad every now and then. Finally, he started to cry and said that he missed his family and could not find them. They told him that I could help him go home. When he got here and discovered I was just a child, he knew I could not help him and was very upset. I remembered what my grandfather had told me about the people and what to do. I started to ask him more questions. I told him about all of my new friends and that there was this light with my new friends that they always seemed to go to and come from. We talked for a long time, and then behind him I could see this light. I thought I was going to get help from Marie – her light was like this whenever I saw her – but Marie did not come. I asked him to turn around and see the light. As he did, he smiled. I could feel him start to shine with joy. He looked at me and said he saw his mother and brother. His mother was calling him, and he had to go now. He turned back around and started walking to this light. I could hear soft music and singing as he slowly faded into the light and heard him say, "thank you."

He was gone, and the light was slowly fading away. I did not know what to do. Did I do the right thing? Was he going to be okay? Then I remembered the beautiful music. I felt tired; my eyes were getting heavy, and I was sleepy. The next morning I awoke, and my cousin was sitting there asking me to get up, that I must be dreaming in my sleep. He heard me last night talking and he wanted to know if I was okay. Grandma had breakfast ready, and I needed to get up and go eat.

Mom came over that day and I tried telling her about Granddaddy New York, how he would come and play with me, and did she know if he went back home yet? My mom got really upset with me and asked me why I would say something like that, that Granddaddy New York was with Jesus in heaven. He was not coming back for any more visits and I should not tell my dad what I told her. I walked away confused and hurt. Why was Mom getting so mad at me? What did I do? I was telling the truth. Wait until he came back. I would tell him what had happened, and then he would fix it. So I sat and waited. He did not come that day, but there was another person waiting for me by the tree, a little girl who had fallen down and gotten sick. When she started to feel better, she was lost and could not find her doggie. Her daddy was gone too, just like her mom. Could I help her find them? I do not remember seeing her before around here, and I asked her where her house was. Did she live down the road? Did she know my mom or grandma? We talked for a little while and then played dolls. We were both getting tired, and she asked me to take her home. When I said that we should go get Grandma, she backed away and said no, only I could help her. That is when I saw the light once again, and it was shining so bright behind her. I told her if she wanted to go home, she needed to go to the light. She started to cry and said if she went there, she would be in trouble for not listening to her mommy. I told her that her mommy was looking for her, and she needed to go so her mommy would not cry any more. We gave each other a hug and promised to see each other again some day. She turned and slowly started to walk to the light and yelled back that she felt funny and happy all at the same time and that her mommy was not mad at her anymore. As the light began to fade away, she was gone.

As I sat with my family playing cards that night, I wondered where my grandfather was and why he did not come to see me today. I started to cry, and my uncle held me in his lap. I told him about my grandfather. He did not seem to know what to say. He just said some people we will never see again and some we will. The ones we see every day love us just as much, and I need to stop playing with pretend people and play more with my real friends. I tried and tried to tell him, but he was just like the rest of them; he still did not believe me. Next thing I know, I was in bed for the night.

I slept through the night, and the next day Grandma was having company. It was okay if I wanted to use the sewing machine to sew more things, but I had to be good and clean up my mess. Grandma's house was always busy as family and friends were always over. I felt like we were the luckiest people around to have so many who came to visit, which meant of course that the cousins all came too. I liked most of them. We were more like brothers and sisters. We played baseball and line-ball, rode bikes and went with Granddaddy to get ice cream. Since I was only a girl and they outnumbered me, I usually came last in the lists of who to play with, which gave me more time to myself and my other friends.

On this day, two friends from down the road came by to play. I really liked them even though they too were boys. I tried to set up the table and teach them school so they could learn what I was learning from my grandfather New York, but they made fun of me and got up to leave. I could not understand why no one believed me or wanted to play. They said I was weird, and they had better friends or better things to do. Grandma came outside to find me sitting on the front porch upset. I told her that I did not feel like doing much and no, I did not care for the boys down the road, they were rude. Grandma went inside and came back out with a bowl. She asked me to help her pick berries, something we all loved to do. I loved the berries that grew along side the yard. We would walk around her whole yard and she would show me how the roses and different flower bushes that she was growing were doing. I told her how much I loved her and that she was the best rose planter, and the angels loved what she did to help them grow. Grandma just laughed and said that she did nothing special, just put the plants in the dirt, and that the roses then knew what to do all by themselves. She just gave them a little help. I asked her if that is what angels do, just give us a little help. She looked at me funny and said, "I am not sure what angels do except for what the bible says, but I am sure they help us."

Then I turned around, and there he was. He was walking across the field with his hat on, and Marie was beside him. I started running, and Grandma stood up and yelled at me to get back so I would not get hurt in the road. I ran back and told her it was okay and that Granddaddy New York was over there and was coming towards us. Grandma got up and looked and then looked back at me and said, "Your mom told you not to tell tales. If you keep it up, you are going to your room." I did not know what to do. She stood there looking at me. I finally said "okay" and walked towards the front door with my head down. Grandma yelled out to me that I could get the broom and sweep the porch if I wanted to. I went in the house and got the broom. As I returned, my grandfather New York and Marie were in the chairs on the front porch. I did not say anything; I was afraid. They just sat there as I swept the porch, and when I was done they told me I had done a great job. I smiled and started talking so fast. I wanted to get everything out before someone else told me I was wrong.

Marie came over and gave me a hug. At that time, I needed one so badly, but my grandfather just sat there. I looked at him, and he said he had something to tell me. He had to be going home because he had some things to do. He could not put it off any longer. He wanted me to understand how much he loved me and how I was such a good brave girl. He said that some things in this life did not seem fair and as I grew up I would understand what he meant. He told me that what people do not seem to understand is that everything in life is fair; we just do not know how to see it. We are all born with the same chance, the same knowing. It is what we do with that knowing that will make us stand out and bring us to the ultimate of what there is to be.

My grandfather picked me up, and we went over to our tree. He said he had a very special gift for me. He told me how proud he was of the help I had given to the people who came to me who needed to go home, that I would see a lot more of them now that I had already helped the other ones. He also said I was being watched over by so many loving beings who were going to walk right beside me for the rest of my life, guiding me along the way. I was to be strong, to always stay true to myself, to love everyone and try to remember not to get upset when people did not believe me. I had a special gift that would give me the ability to see the truth in people, to help heal Mother Earth and her people and bring a truth to the light of all situations. I came from a long line of noble wise ones, and Mother one day would call me to be in service and what a great honor that will be. He said that Marie was my guardian angel. She would help me in whatever I needed as long as I was a good girl, and she would help me find him when I needed to. He looked so sad, but he felt so warm, rich, and so full of what I could feel of the light that always showed up. I snuggled close to him and told him I loved him. He kissed the top of my head and said he would always be there for me and loved me like the stars that shine. He had to go as he could hear his name called by his son, and his son he loved beyond forever. When I looked back up, my grandfather was gone. Marie was smiling so bright and said, "Your grandfather has done such good work in these times. He will be close. He has opened the doors for you, and that took much strength. He now needs to be at hand to help heal a broken heart." Marie waved goodbye as she turned away and said she would see me tomorrow, and that I best go in and eat dinner before I get in trouble with my grandmother.

Two years later, after my sixth birthday, I was playing with my friends. We were running through my grandmother's house. I was turning a corner and was yelled at by my uncle to watch where I was going, and by the way, what was I doing? Well, I was playing tag with my friend. My uncle looked at me and asked whom I was playing with. When I told him, he went off on something about how I needed to stop lying and to go outside to play with the other kids. He would go find Mom or Grandma. At those moments, my friends would move the walls once again and go right through, so of course I took up where we left off and try to tag them again. This was the best of games. The best hiding place, of course, was the closet under the stairs. To get there, I would go through my grandfather's wardrobe. It always smelled like him and he would have clothes hanging up on the left side, so I would push the clothes out of the way and go to the back and step right through the wall. Sometimes I would be found through the normal door (as we called it) and be told to get out of there in an instant.

This day was so much fun. After we were done playing, I ran outside to see what everyone else was doing. My brother and cousin were playing line-ball. You stood under the power utility line attached to the house. You scored by how you threw the ball and if it hit the utility lines. I asked them if I could play. Some days they would just say okay but really try to ignore me other days. Of course, when they told me no, I would get so upset that if I did not tell Grandma I would go sit under my tree and just think. This day, as I started towards my tree, I looked up and there he was, my Grandfather New York was there waiting. I ran so hard I was out of breath when I got there. I could not believe it. Where had he been, and why had he not come back in all this time? Then it did not matter – he was here, and I had missed him. I told him so much of everything and anything, trying to get it all out before he could leave. He promised me he was here to visit for a short while and that he had been around; he just had a lot of work he had been doing while he was away. He told me that he had a special visitor for me to meet, the lady he had told me about so long ago. I told him I had waited and watched but she never came. After he stopped laughing, he told me that she had been around watching me all this time and that she was very proud of me. I stood there with my mouth open, not knowing what to say. I do not remember seeing a lady as he had said, but I would pay closer attention.

Just then a beautiful butterfly floated by. He asked me about the butterfly, and I told him all I knew on how they changed their looks as a caterpillar by going inside a cocoon until they hatched themselves into a beautiful butterfly. He looked thoughtful and then smiled and said that I had done very well with my school lessons. He explained the process of how a caterpillar in their own transformation inside the cocoon was, of course then re-born into the most beautiful of God's creatures. He applied this to what we as humans go through and do not recognize. He told me how Marie had kept him up to date with all of the birthdays and friends. She was having so much fun with me. I love Marie; she had become my very best friend. As I looked around, three balls of light came floating by; and then three ladies were standing beside us at the tree. "I remember them," I told my grandfather. These three are the angelic ones whom I met a long time ago. He told me yes, they are the angelic wise ones. I was a part of them as much as they were a part of me, and they are to work with me and teach me how to heal things. I was not sure what healing was except that when I hurt myself Grandma and Granddaddy would take me to the doctor. They said the doctor was going to make me feel better and that was healing, right? Yes, he said, but this was a different kind of healing. I would be taking my hands and place them on living things, and they would heal. He said it was a matter of allowing myself to see the light within, and letting the light shine through me to the living thing that I was to heal. Then it would be healed and feel so much better. He told me the story of Jesus, how Jesus was such a gentle loving light who healed so many living things and that in time I would too. He said it is not so much what I do but what I allow to be done through me as I kept myself truthful in all things. He told me how important it was to love Jesus and how Jesus loved me, as I was a child of God. Now, he had me confused. It sounded so right, so right that my heart warmed when I thought of it. Still, I had a daddy; wasn't Daddy his son? Yes, my grandfather said; but even my daddy, his son, is a child of God. It took all the rest of the time we had that day for him to help me remember who I was. When he did, he shined so bright; he was brighter than the sun.

My brothers and cousins were all staying over that day. We would all get together like this often, and what grand adventures we would have. I met my grandfather and the angelic wise ones for what seemed like forever and learned how to heal plants, trees, birds, frogs and flowers. I could even place my hands on myself and help heal the pain and hurt when I fell. My grandfather told me what a good student I was in the learning school, and that now I would have to learn how to place my hands on other people to help heal them too. The funny part was I knew I had done this before. I could see the times and people in my dreams when I would go and touch them and they would get up as if nothing was wrong. I remember when people were scared of what others could do with this healing, how they would tell on those who placed their hands on others and they would be healed, and how when the ones who could heal and would help to heal others were out after dark, they were taken away; I would never see them again.

I remember one night when I fell asleep on the couch in Grandma's living room. The next thing I knew, I was flying and then I would be outside of her house looking in through the front door and windows. I would fly up the hill to the neighbors and watch as they were having a party in the house. I would fly to my great aunt's house next door and see her sleeping as my great uncle was in the kitchen getting a glass of water. Later, when I told my grandfather about this, he would explain that I had been out of my body flying around and visiting. If I kept it up, I could go to other places on earth and whole other worlds and see everything I wanted. He told me to be very careful with this. If someone came in my bedroom and touched me, it would jolt me back in my body too fast and I could get sick. However, if I asked my angels and guides, they would keep me safe until I returned. I looked forward to each night that I could go out and explore. I visited my family and other places so much that my family would question me during the day about how I knew what was going on over there in someone else's house when it was happening while I was in bed. The would say it was impossible for me to know any of it; I must have been listening to someone's conversations. Then I would get in trouble once again for telling the truth. This was very confusing for me; I just could not understand what the problem was with everyone.

One very pretty day, I knew something wonderful was going to happen. It was almost my seventh birthday, and the spring flowers were staring to come up. No one stopped by Grandma's today except for the ice cream man. When I would hear his music coming from way far away, I would make my grandmother stand out by the road forever to get some ice cream cones. This was my favorite treat of all time, and we would sit on the front porch. She would tell me the stories of her family, and we would talk about all the music we loved. Today was special, and I could feel it everywhere around me. I went to the bathroom and, as I was coming out, I ran right into my Grandfather New York. He was standing there looking in the large mirror in the hallway. He looked so handsome today; he felt it too, I just knew it. He held out his hand and said, "Come on, I have that surprise for you now." We went outside and stood by Grandma's garden. She worked very hard on her garden every day, and she always grew the best tomatoes. My grandfather told me to be polite, for we were going to have a special visitor. I asked him how he knew, and he said he was told from a friend to be here at this time. When he found a place of love, it would be the right time. Well, this garden was a place of love but so was my tree, so were the lilacs, and so was – I knew now that the most favorite place of love for me is the willow tree with its long arms that sweep me up and that blows gently in the wind. This tree is my friend. I helped heal it, and she loves me as much as I love her.

I started running, and when I got to this tree, my grandfather was already there waiting. He told me how bright I was, and yes, I had chosen well. As we were standing there, in the very center of the tree was a brilliant blue light with sparks of gold flying out. In the center of the light was a lady, a magnificent lady that I knew, I knew her, my heart knew her. I started to cry from the overwhelming love that she was sending me. I went over to her, and she touched my face. I could feel her love as she spoke to me. She said she missed me and how good it was to see me once again. She wanted to make sure I was happy and ready, as I had promised her. I remember nodding yes and aching from the longing inside of me to be that close to her again. This is Mother, the Blessed Mother, the Divine being of all; she is here once again with me. Mother proceeded to talk to me, to tell me what I am here to do, how at the time I will awaken to follow her words to help the whole of the consciousness of all living creatures on Mother Earth. From this day forward, I will go and finish this school of knowledge. I will learn as they all learn. I will go through many trials and tribulations, for I have chosen to be blinded to the light until such time as she awakens me to her presence to do her work as she decrees. At the time of decision, I shall be a true clear avatar of knowledge and ascend to her side.

I drew closer to her as she held me in her arms. As we touched, I embraced the light so pure I knew that I would not feel it again for many an earth year. My grandfather stood proud beside me. I could feel it move all over me. He gently held my hand and said he too must go, but that he would be forever near and that when I felt alone to call to him and he would be there. I sat down on the bottom of the tree trunk and cried. I felt so alone and empty inside. I knew I had so many things to do, but here I was so little and so young. I had many earth years to go, as Mother had said. How long that would be, I did not know. I was in this earth body and so alone. When my tears dried up, I stood up and looked around. No one was there; I was being given the time to think about everything. I ran to the house just in time to have dinner: Grandma's fried chicken, mashed potatoes and gravy. It was the type of old-fashioned love in the first bite you take, crispy skin with just the hint of salt to bring out the flavor of the gravy that is smothered over her mashed potatoes, this was my favorite food that Grandma would make. All of it just melts in your mouth as the flavors blend together. As kids, we would fight over who got the chicken leg. My cousin and I would have to take turns with that one. Somehow, I always seemed to be the one whose turn it would be the next time. What Grandma would do was save me a piece for later when no one else was around. That night with a full belly, I would have no dreams, just a peaceful night's sleep until the next day when I would play once again with my friends and run through the walls only to be told to stop and go outside.

I share these experiences with you, for perhaps you can see yourself. I seemed to always get in trouble from that moment on. The more I worked with spirit, the more no one believed me or wanted me around. I was too weird, and I talked to people who were not there and whom everyone else could not see. Over the next couple of years, the nighttime visitors got so crowded in my bedroom that I finally had to tell them to stop. I could not get any sleep at night, and they needed to stay out of my bedroom. I would sleep with the lights on and a "Do Not Disturb" sign, and I would pull the shades all the way down. At times, I could still see them peaking between the windowsill and the shades. I want to say on this note, if your children tell you they see spirit – please believe them. You do not have to go overboard but ask them to tell you about them, to draw a picture of them, anything so that they learn their own self worth. Every time I would see spirit, I learned how to tell a lie about the truth of seeing them so I would not get in trouble with my family and friends. Then I would have to learn how to tell what people wanted to hear, which for them was the truth but I knew it was a lie. This is the most confusing place to be for any child. They have enough going on in their young lives dealing with these gifts and abilities, trying to have friends, trying to fit in, trying to understand what in the world is going on around them. Do not push them. They know who they are; they just need to understand and remember why they are! These children have no ego; they have no heart for glory and fame. They are here to serve and do their work, and they will have all they need to see them through, that I promise you.

My grandfather opened the doors for me that night so long ago. I did not understand all of it then; it was so simple that it is just a part of who I was. I did not feel special or that I was different from anyone else. To me, I was like everyone else and everyone else was like me. I would tell people about the ones I would see around them, or what was going to be happening soon in their lives, and that is when I slowly learned – I am alone. I am alone in the world as no other, and I did not want to be here and be alone. I wanted to go home, home where I was accepted for who I was, loved for what I was doing that was as natural as taking a breath, loved for being me.

So love your children and watch the friends they are close with. Do not look at their friends as my old friends and their families looked at me. The children come in all sizes and colors. They come from all backgrounds and ethnic groups. They come humbly and lovingly to help each other. They are respectful and humble; they are shy and bold. They know their own self worth, and when they are being judged they will stand up and not judge back but send you love.

With these words, I wanted you to look and see what is actually going on with you in your childhood, from the past and up to this present moment. Sit down and remember when...when you were that child and find a special memory of that time. Go back to the faces of those around you. Recognize as many as you can; do you see? Then start to piece the pieces together. Look at the faces of those who you physically remember, family and friends. Pull that warmth of love into your heart. Now look at the faces between the crowds of your physical loved ones, and you can smile deeply when you recognize those in spirit of those who were also with you each day as a guide, angel or teacher. You will be amazed at what was going on the whole time and that, yes, you too were always open to them.

Chapter II

LESSONS FROM THE OLD SCHOOL

This I have to say is the most interesting of all things to look at in our lives for those who already are or who aspire to become mediums and psychics as part of their spiritual development. It will also be of interest to you if you have any experiences with psychics or mediums on your journey, and you want to understand more about these helpers.

As we approach these times we live in each day and the future events that are about to unfold, you must understand and know about the Old School verses New School and the feelings associated with it. Old School mediums are those who came before you as in anything. These are the forerunners of our time, the ones who paid their dues and worked so very long and hard through the era when people believed what was in front of them all the way to the dis-belief of a hoax being presented to them. The old schoolers have learned how to keep their business to themselves and to be very weary about nosy newcomers wanting to hang around.

Now, no one really talks about this side of a medium/psychic's world. It is like an unwritten rule, and, of course, I can only tell you what I receive as a visionary and what I personally experienced. The number one rule is "never talk bad about another medium!" Very simple. You may describe them. You may refer others to go to them for a reading or session, but you never want to judge another by saying their name in a harmful way.

Most of today's mediums and or psychics have had some experiences with Spiritualist camps. These camps are in different areas around the world. Others have never heard of these camps, and that is okay. Spiritualist camps are the places where one is drawn to learn about mediumship and developing their gifts and or abilities. I bring them to your awareness as something new or something that you too have had experiences with, and yes, it is all different from one individual to the next.

I am not going to go headlong into the social or political processes of the spiritualist camps, as I know there are books out in society that deal with this more than what my goal is here. I also do not hang around spiritualist camps. Yes, I have visited them. I have taken workshops and participated in classes and séance circles, but I have not studied under one in a totality, as I am not to be a part of that sector. It does not mean that I was not to go and learn what I needed to see and experience, just as you will have the choice to see if it is right for you. My guides, angels and teachers have kept me away from being so enthralled in these spiritualist camps in any way that I lose my own self. I am a spiritual individual not a spiritualist. There is a huge difference among us as there is also a warm familiarity.

The information that I am talking about regarding old schoolers does deal with a small area of these camps and that is why I am giving my take on them. I do recommend if you ever have the chance to go and visit a Spiritualist Camp, enjoy all they have to offer, this is the best way for you to see for yourself what these Camps are all about. You will meet a surprising amount of mediums who live and visit these camps that will be warm and welcoming, gifted and talented. There are two types of spiritualist camps: one is in physical mediumship and the other is in mental mediumship. All of the camps have their own Declaration of Principles and at least one major goal in common "to prove the continuity of Life" in what their own by-laws describe as the continuity of life and the communication with deceased loved ones who are in spirit. This is the foundation of what a medium's expectations are to the given public arena. Spiritualism as a movement began long before the Fox family in 1848, and it has since become both a religion, and more of a science and philosophy. Both have their own declarations in which all who are a member of their established churches follow.

In the heyday of psychics and mediums, both camps did produce physical manifestations, as you can read their own history by purchasing their historical books at the camps or local bookstores. They give detailed descriptions of all that went on through the life, times and growth of the spiritualist camps, their own evolution. Over the years, all of the camps have had their own shadows of individuals who would come in to find out the "deep dark secrets" of their camps, to debunk in any way, shape or form. As history goes, some were proven false and some were not. I can lay no claim as to the authenticity of any of these camps as I am not a member, and it is not my job. I look at it this way...if I can do all the things with my own gifts and abilities then so can another, and it is not for me to call them out in what they do. I am here to bring the truths to the children of God and to assist and guide them to their own spiritual awakening of their true authentic selves.

There is mental mediumship that only deals with the giving of a message from your loved ones in spirit. Those from the spiritualist camps of mental mediumship, ones that I have dealt with in the past, do not want to hear about guides, teachers and definitely not angels of any shape, color or form. Only through a message from your loved ones in spirit, can there be any confirmation of the continuity of life. This makes it clean, easy and straightforward to the receiver of any spirit communication. I have many friends who are both mental and physical mediums who work very hard in what they do, and I respect them for being the vehicle to which those messages may be delivered to others.

With physical mediumship, the mediums will prove the continuity of life through mental mediumship and physical objects that are given to the individuals during readings, séance circles of trance mediumship, spirit card writings, trumpet circles, smoke billets etc. It is the touching of a physical object from the departed loved one that the medium can then give you your messages with Psychometry, which I will talk about later. Now, I love physical mediumship as this is one I identify with most. Yes, we receive messages from your loved ones in the mental way, but to open it up even more to produce something that you may have and to hold onto means so much and can open up your heart for the peace, healing and closure you may need.

I do spirit art, which is where I will sit with a pad of paper and drawing supplies and then meditate. As I meditate, I allow spirit to move through me to use the drawing pens that I have to draw a picture of themselves, other individuals, guides, teachers, angels; a whole host of ones to let me know who is around, how they are doing and what they look like. I do sessions where the physical individuals will sit in front of me and their guides or loved ones in spirit will come through and working with one of my artist guides I will go into a slight trance, after making that connection the guides will then come through and utilizing the drawing materials that I have before me, will assist in drawing a self portrait of themselves to give to their loved one here in the physical. We will then have a picture for them to see and take home with them. This is a very emotional and powerful time. A lot of times this is to give confirmation to the individual that yes, you are true and correct in what you are going through, what you see and are experiencing. In addition, most of the times it is emotional when they will pull a picture out of their wallet to show me the comparison of the spirit portrait and one taken when the loved one was physically alive. In almost everything I do, there is physical evidence or something physical that I can touch or see with, to then open the doors to others in the spiritual realms and assist them to deliver loving messages to their loved one here in the physical.

Now between these two different sectors of the spiritualist camps, they will have members who will discount the other camps. This has been an internal war of words, works and abilities for a very long time now. It makes it so hard and confusing for the individual who just wants to learn. I believe that no side is the best side; it is up to what calls and attracts you the individual as to which direction and spiritualist camp you want to visit. Like most of my friends, you will go to both types of spiritualist camps just for the experience even though you will enjoy yourself, you will also feel the tension and come away with a favorite place that will always be in your heart, how can you not? When it all comes down to everything, we must always remember we are all one in God's eyes. There should be no sides when we are all here to lovingly assist one another. Why does there need to be a choosing of sides?

These two very alike but different spiritualist camps have been losing their public following. There will still be crowded summers and weekends, but the trend of going back is wearing thin as these two go head to head in a battle they are clearly out to win. But they don't see what is lost along the way.

In the past few years especially in what I see, both of these sectors of camps have been losing clients and potential students while trying to get the best talent of mediums through their doors to attract the clients and students to them. They hold special weekends when they promise the best talents and yes, they do get the best of gifted mediums. Then when these special individuals are gone, they have another problem. Their teachers, most but not all of them, are being too selective on who they want to work with as a student. They want the student there to learn, but as the student steps up and has a truly amazing connection with spirit and is stepping into their own gifts and abilities, the teacher will crush it so the student will have to continue going back. They have their favorites, as in all areas of life. It reminds you of grade school when you knew who the teacher's pet was. What they fail to realize is that people notice.

I once took some of my students to a séance circle. When it was over, I expressed my enthusiasm to one of the teachers about how I was bringing all of these students and more to a weekend workshop series. This teacher looked at me and said, "NO, they are not ready." I stood there a minute and said "okay," as all of my students heard this. I walked away thinking, *you just ruined a great time of learning and experience for future mediums.* This was to be a weekend workshop open to the public in which I knew there were going to be individuals with less learning than my own students. The biggest problem I could see was that this teacher knew what I was capable of and that these students then too were going to be great mediums in their own rights, not just from what I teach them but also for who they themselves were and how they would apply all that they learn. I am just a vehicle to give all of what I have to the student, it is then up to the student to apply that in which they learn.

All of these problems add up, and after awhile all you have to do is sit back and watch the energy play out as to how these camps have lost the gain they had so long ago. They will always be there, but the times are changing and will not always support them if they themselves do not move forward to reach out to those who need their knowledge. These camps across the world have much to offer and give to those who seek them out, for it all is in the direction that they apply themselves to give to others. Years gone by with the energies that we had with and around us could take years to become a medium, not today, in this energy we have around us what took twenty years for the old schoolers is only taking five to ten for the newbies, we need to recognize this and stay on top of the energy also. Bring out the best in all and the best shall come from you.

The reason I tell you all this is for you to know what is out there and to understand in which direction to go and to know what to expect as you do so. As in all things, I love the fact that there are the different spiritualist camps across the world to bring a true understanding and learning to all. It is in the history of those before you that you become that much more to those around you today.

As a visionary, I have been shown things like this from many years ago. I was told by the Blessed Mother and the Angelic Wise Ones that I and others like me were going to be offering a new school of learning. All I needed would be shown to me, and I was to give all of it to others:

"We are here to share and teach those searching for who they are, why they are here and their spiritual paths. We come now before the time when the doors are opening to all those who choose to seek the knowledge that is their 'birth-right' to have access to them.

A teaching of development that is new to you and very old to us. We are here to assist you, Adele, in opening their eyes to spirit across the veil and their communication with us. Do they not feel there is something missing in their life? Do they not seek something their heart is calling for too? Do they wonder who they are, and why they are here?"

To this day I am here teaching as much as I can to as many as I can. It is a mission I signed up for from the very beginning, and, as I said earlier, if I can assist you in discovering who you are, my mission is complete. So in keeping with old school knowledge of what we went through because, yes, I consider myself old school with a twist of new, I give you these growing years.

To understand all of this, I need to explain a little history of the everyday psychic and medium, keeping in mind this is from my own personal history. When I was growing up, there were no bookstores to go to, to look up all of these gifts or abilities for a reference of understanding and to help develop them, unlike the many resources that you have been blessed with today. Back then, you had the local library. Many of the local everyday libraries did not carry those books that did not go with societies dictates on what we should now and what we should not. If you were lucky, you could find a handful of books in the "Occult" section. Moreover, not knowing about the many great and gifted individual mediums as we do now, I am sure there was a book about Madame Blavatsky, but being one who did not know what to look for to describe what was going on, I would not of known to look her up to find something to read. You would stand in the aisle in front of the books and, if you did not care what people thought of you, you would stay in front of the section you were browsing in. Otherwise, you would turn your back and pretend you were looking up something else. As for me, it didn't matter. I wanted to understand and find the best information I could, even though the ladies in the library would stare and wonder what in the world this young lady was doing, looking up something in the Occult section. In a small town, it was easy for everyone to know the other person's business. We seemed to be well known for the size of our family and the fact that my mother worked at the local grocery store. As the years went by I would see others in the book sections looking for all of this on spiritualism and they would grab a few books and hide around the corner to be able to read them. I love going into a local bookstore now and seeing it filled with individuals seeking books on these same subjects and actually asking for assistance in what they need.

I never really found anything when I was younger that I could say helped me one way or the other to find out what these gifts and abilities were, what I needed to do next or what to expect from them. Most books were on magicians or the darker side of the light, so I would just blow out my breath and walk away, and head home to read the bible. As you know, this is the oldest book on psychics, mediums, prophets and healers. I did not always agree with what was written as I read the pages but it was reassuring just to know that there was a book that I was told to read, one that was honored and very important to just about everyone. Here was a book that talked about things that I understood and could work with, as in this chapter of *Corinthians 1, Gifts from the Holy Spirit*. Incredible to think that all these years you search, and here it was under your nose the whole time!

Now remember, The things that I could do or where going on around me was not the kind of information that you would go to church or school and just talk to everyone about. You learned what to mention and what not to mention. However, I do remember one beautiful girl in high school who was into a lot of this in more of a white wicca way. I would just watch her and keep quiet, but I was fascinated to see her wanting to learn something that she was interested in that everyone kind of mocked her for (even though she did not publicize it to everyone) and then watching her results. She was learning to be a true alchemist. At the time, I do not think she knew this to the fullest extent. Ten years later, I ran into her; she glowed from the inside out. I could see that she had accomplished her goals!

Now as we could not fully advertise ourselves, as a medium, psychic , healer, etc.. those of us who were young, closed ourselves off from individuals in their own infancy of life. I was in fact, made fun of and called numerous times a freak, weird or a witch. I often wondered if those who said the names actually knew what the words meant and how they were affecting my life by their own actions. And when I did close up to keep my own counsel they were in fact assisting me into becoming weirder in the eyes of the public realms. In finding others like myself who had these gift and connections with spirit was fun and uplifting. With all of this new insight of meeting other individuals who were gifted as myself I was introduced to the séances circle rooms, where we then took our work into the basements and pallor rooms of friends and associates. I have been going to séances since I was very young, so it was exciting to finally find a place where I could be with others who could do what I could do. To be excepted and not be a freak. It was almost an elite club of sorts. There were no dues, just a love offering and sometimes not even that as we were among those of like mind and welcomed to just be there. You were only permitted to be there if you were personally invited to these séances, and the only way you knew or would find out anything about these séance circles was by word of mouth. As we would gather in the circle, sometimes sitting with a table between us and touching fingertips, we would all say a prayer of protection, you could then feel the energy moving from one individual to another around the circle. It was exciting for me when the chosen medium would call in and invite those in spirit to join us and make their presence known. This is the point where you hold your breath as you wait for what will happen next. Sometimes someone would jump and say, "They are here," and everyone's energy would raise another level as we watched and listened. Sometimes the chosen medium would then be thrown back and start speaking the words of the one in spirit who was with us.

Sometimes nothing would happen; those nights the room would be quiet. On those nights as we gathered to leave, individuals would be a little disappointed, but everyone understood that what is meant to be will be and that is what the séance circle is about.

The greatest experience to me was when I was with one level or another of individuals in their development and they were experimenting with the energies of spirit and learning to work with their gifts (as we were always testing our own selves) to know that spirit was standing right there. No one seemed to be connecting with them. I would just smile and watch and know in my heart that we did make contact; it was just that the chosen medium had not opened themselves up enough to make the contact, or it was not meant to be at that moment in time. Sometimes you would sit in a circle or area and watch the channel do their work; this is one who allows spirit to come through and uses their voice box and physical body to act as a conduit of energy. This was always amazing to be a part of; the channeled energy of the spirit would either talk to everyone or sometimes stop and direct a message to a certain individual. Of course, I learned that we are all channels in one form or another. As with being a psychic, medium or healer, it is up to the individual to develop and work with the ability and gift they have and choose which direction to take it in.

Those who I chose to be around in these séances were truly gifted. They would shine as I could see their master teachers in the spiritual realms beside them, the glorious angels with their arms around them, loving them. These were wonderful times of my growing years. Most of the participants I did not know. We were not there to be the best of friends; we were there to witness and be a part of the experience. We all choose in which direction to go in our lives.

Sometimes the choices we make are not always the correct ones at that time, and when this happens, we find ourselves saying, "I learned that the hard way."

You will likely sit in many circles, classes or modern forms of séances. I was fortunate enough to be a part of a group of individuals at one time who were all truly gifted. As we came together, we had a young lady who opened her home to us. We would meet and sit to develop our gifts; those were some great nights being together and seeing what we could of one another. As time went on, we all knew when it was time to walk away to move forward in another area. You will find that some circles are like that. You are there for an extended period of time to learn and gather all that there is for you, and then there will be a time when you will walk away, knowing that you learned some valuable lessons to take with you since this is just another stage to your spiritual development. That's why I say you should honor all before and after you, for one day that walk may bring you back to them again.

Then you have it at the other end. Once, as a teenager, I was asked to go to a gathering at a local hotel meeting room. I guess my family believed that they needed some help to understand what to do with me, what was going on with me, that I needed some type of intervention and this was worth a try. At the time, there was a growing movement to follow the understanding and teachings from what I then understood was a well known psychic by the name of Jean Dixon. In this meeting, I was told, there would be women who would listen to her tapes and then get together to discuss her work. I found out this was the farthest from the truth, for it was actually a Christian based chapter of the Woman's Aglow that had nothing to do with listening to tapes of future events.

It went like this. I arrived at this hotel, and I walked into the meeting room with the individual who brought me.

As I looked around, I saw rows of chairs filled with women who all wore large necklaces of crosses. They were all just staring at me as we entered, as anyone could tell I was a newbie. Then the sermon started, and the next thing I know I was in this zone of hazy light around me. A protection of sorts for me to see the truth of the situation that I was in. As I sat there, these ladies were all staring and beckoning the sinner to come forward to be cleansed of the evil inside, to throw their self forward and be whole in the sight of God. This kept up for so long I finally realized they were talking about me. Oh my goodness. They were trying to speak in what is known as "tongues," and at that point I could see their "ugly side" coming out and closing in around me. It was as if I was being surrounded on all sides from a bunch of hunters who were ready to strike at any moment. Even though they believed they were speaking in tongues, I knew they were not. I just sat there in total confusion, knowing in my heart that there was no way I was a sinner and was going to get down on my knees to these ladies. Just then, my guardian angel stood in front of me and said, "Just keep the prayer of God in your heart and nothing will happen," and that is just what I did. I asked for the Light of God to enter upon me and surround me in the comforting arms of the Holy Spirit. I could feel this amazing amount of energy surround me and hold me tight, a warmth that spread through me. I had the Love of God with me, and nothing then could happen to me. After a long period of time, as those up on the podium and around me tried their hardest to get me to come forward, it was over. I stood up and finally walked out.

This experience left me in a daze at first; I had to get away and cleanse that energy from me. Then I had to laugh. Here was my first experience with what I would call an occult. I was still in shock for many days later. I do believe these ladies truly believed in what they were doing; they were just a little misguided in the purpose of what they do. They were opening up to what they believed was an extension of their own church beliefs. If I had not been strong in my own knowing and listening to my guardian angel, I feel as if they would have dragged me up to the podium to drill what they perceived as evil from me.

I share this story with you for you to see what a traumatic experience this could be for anyone at any age as they come into their own spirituality, and how society sees things differently from its own perceptions. Yes, I was a child who was going through learning my identification of who I was and how to fit in among my own peers, but I didn't need to be put through an experience like this. If anything, it would scare someone away from all things related to church or spirituality. For me, it reaffirmed the importance of the only thing I truly had to do, which was to call upon the Light of God. There is no greater power than God's Light. Embrace the Light, and it will embrace you always and forever.

I come from love when I describe all of this. I honor the Old School psychics and mediums, those who are the forerunners in this wonderful area of our own connection to the spiritual realms, to learn and understand that all of these individuals learned from that which was learned the hard way, by trial and error of living with it each day of their lives, to working with their gifts and abilities in less than perfect surroundings and concealing that which they are to society but also standing with courage to bring awareness to everyone at their own peril. They have earned their acknowledgement in this work and world; they have, as I say, "paid their dues" and opened the doors for all future psychics and mediums to walk through.

Love and blessings, a gratitude of thanks, are sent to you as those who walk behind you find the door you have left open for them to walk through in their own development and spiritual journey. Until you look into the face of someone and say, "I am a medium," you cannot realize the terror or the joy and fascination that can truly run through someone's being. I have to laugh as I remember when I would gently tell an acquaintance, the mother to one of my daughter's friends, that "I am a medium." They would immediately try to look interested and ask what I meant and then the realization of what it meant would hit them square in the face. Their eyes go blank; they would purse their lips together. And then it was there, as you can see their thoughts running in their heads, "Oh my goodness, is she reading me right now? What does she know about me? I always thought there was something odd about her." Their whole facial structure would change, and they could not wait to get away. I would talk a few more minutes and then walk away with a large smile on my face. Later, when I would see them again, they would turn around and walk in the opposite direction. Now this is their choice, of course, as they only know that which has been taught to them by the conditioning of society.

So much of the earlier years of my life was filled with individuals who chose not to know me by who I was but what they only wanted to believe. I would send them love and just kept doing what I was doing. You see, you bless those who would hurt you or not want to understand you, for they do not know what they judge. You send no judgment to them, for who are you to judge or cast the first stone?

Because of those kinds of experiences I had, I especially honor all of the Newbies today, for they have opened up to their spiritual awakening. Many things are going on around them; they are having experiences that they do not understand. They are trying to seek answers and not finding something solid they can hold onto.

There are those who are willing to teach, but are there those who are willing to go the extra mile and teach all they know? Yes, there are; use your discernment when choosing that teacher for yourself. I teach that what is given to me to give to others. I am here to teach right from wrong even if I find myself walking that thin line in doing so, as I assist others in waking up and tweaking away the illusions that society has dictated, to bring a love for all things as they open themselves to their own gifts and abilities, to bring this awareness to all God's children great or small. There is no judgment to anyone, for we are all in this together and together we must stand as a united front in the light of God. If your heart is crying out with that which you do not understand, then I am here to help to my best ability. We all are learning; there is not one single day that goes by that we do not learn something new to add to who we are. With this, I introduce you next to the Newbies and Sleepers.

CHAPTER III

NEWBIES AND SLEEPERS

I said this in the Introduction, and it's so important that I'll say it again. Nine out of ten people you know are having a spiritual awakening, and they don't even realize it. They are in contact with spirit each day; but because of society's conditioning, they are clueless to all of it.

You know who I am talking about, the individual who is having the nervous breakdown, anxiety attacks, depression, relationship problems and a huge feeling of their body being in a rush to get somewhere as if something is about to happen. They cannot figure out what. As a society, the individuals seek that which can help them with all they are going through, whether it is the use of medicine or other alternatives. Or, just the opposite, they are having a knowing that this is something spiritual but do not understand what that means or what to do next. What they are asking for on any level within their being is an understanding as to why they are going through it all in the first place.

So to all of you, I say, "Welcome, let me invite you into the learning process of your spiritual journey." The first thing I teach all of my students is about Newbies and Sleepers, which is "old school and new school." This is information that to me is very essential in your learning, what you need to understand, that you are beginning a journey of recognition, remembrance and then knowing. You need a foundation on which to stand. Without that foundation as in any structure, you will fall.

By the time a new student sits down in one of my classes, I know which they are, a newbie or sleeper, and why they are with me, what they need to learn, where they need to go and what they need to do. I notice if they:

- Are fresh and new to all things spiritual
- Are starting to or are seeing something when nothing and no one is there
- Are starting to or are hearing conversations when no one is there
- Have a knowing of things that they cannot explain
- Are experiencing deja vu
- Are having experiences at night that frighten them
- Are having dreams that are getting stronger and showing bizarre things to them
- Report having been to a psychic or medium who tells them they are gifted
- Share a story about an encounter with an angelic being
- Find themselves being able to all of a sudden look at someone and see a spirit form beside them
- Are seeing something in the peripheral line of vision
- Are having a nervous breakdown
- Lack a foundation of knowledge in the field of psychics and mediumship
- Come from having a few years of spiritual learning
- Carry some knowledge of astrology, healing modalities or meditations
- Feel that their whole being is in a rush to go somewhere

These are truly some awareness signs of a soul being spiritually awakened as if all of this has been deep within them, and they are not understanding what in the world to do with it or what in the world is going on. They talk to their friends who look cross-eyed at them and start to laugh, or their spouse is thinking their loved one is whacked out and then ignores the whole thing. They go to bookstores and try to find anything that can help them. They find psychics or mediums to visit and acquire readings from to help them understand. They look for a group or gathering where they will find other like-minded individuals who will not stare at them funny. When they start to slow down to breathe, the teacher arrives and you think, *Finally, I need someone to help me understand all of this crazy stuff.*

Now, some come into their awakening by way of auto accidents, physical accidents, nervous breakdowns and surgeries or any traumatic experience. This is what I really call a "wake-up call!" The wake-up call you have received is just that: "Hello, wake up, and get to work!" This happens when you have reached a part of this physical experience that you are to be working with your gifts and abilities to understand them, but you are or have been just ignoring them. The Universe and God find a way to get you to pay attention to that which you are here to do.

All of a sudden, you find yourself at a loss for all of the things that you are now able to do: seeing, hearing, sensing, feeling, smelling and knowing about things and people around you. With an urge to do something that you cannot explain, you start to think differently. You see how things that you use to love seem to be falling away from you. Your friends and family start to whisper or communicate as they have always done; you are just truly watching and listening to them and seeing everyone in a different light. If your family is the gossiping or confrontational type, you start to back away. When you are asked to do things that you used to like, you beg out of going. Your whole world is opening in a new way, and you are just adjusting. You have a sudden awareness of really knowing about all things spiritual, trying to find where you belong and what exactly that you are connected to in all things.

Newbies have a tremendous amount of love in their awakening, and they share with others in one way or another. They just do not have the knowledge of the spiritual realms with them. They know who they are and can and will do great things in whatever direction they go. With this, the newbies must watch the ego level they are working with.

Sleepers

Old School, psychics, mediums, healers, channels, astrologers, you know them, all of those whom everyone talked about. You would occasionally visit to let them tell you about who you are and what is going on in your life. "Will I change my job soon?" "Will I find the man of my dreams?" "Will I win the lottery?" These are individuals of the old school, ones who subconsciously led you to believe they were the only gifted ones around, ones who would tell you that yes, this will happen or no, that will happen. Sometimes they were right, and sometimes they were close to being right. I honor them, for they were the forerunners to us all.

One thing they almost always did was lead you to believe no one other than themselves could know your future or tell your future; no one else could talk to your deceased loved ones. Sleepers did not share!!! Oh, they made you believe they did. They did not want to share everything with you, for then, you see, you would know as much as they did.

What I call old school mediumship is where you had an individual who was gifted and who worked hard at showing you how gifted they were. They did not share their knowledge of the gift to the point where you might become better than they were. If you became better than them, you were no longer allowed in the inner circle. Their own ego could not deal with this; they honored you inside of themselves but hesitated to do so publicly. Over a period of time, they were placed in a somewhat *sleeping* mode of their gifts and abilities. Some kept working as they sat on the fence and did try to show others a few things, but only what they wanted them to learn to then be a student to assist them with their psychic or medium abilities and to further their own personal work with their students.

Others were quiet in their work with spirit; they got too far away from what they were supposed to be doing. They did not feel or see why they should share all of what they knew, and the gift that they had once had came to a halt. The lower energy has a way of sneaking up on someone who is not looking or not being in integrity with who they are. Their abilities to be that gifted with their work were taking its toll on them. They did not do half of what we do today in our work with clearing, cleansing, sharing and loving. They really were not supposed to, to a certain degree, for they had their own learning to do with all of it. They took steps too far out on a limb; they would do things that they believed they could do with limited preparation because of who they were, and then the gift would eventually turn on them.

When I was younger, my aunt used to do Tarot in her space of my grandmother's house. At other times, she would be at a friend's house. She was a lovey. She was very good, but because family and friends gave her a hard time, she stopped what she was doing. When she would do a séance or reading, I would be there and watch spirit come around. They would show me things and do some pretty funny or scary anecdotes that no one else seemed to be aware of. Oh, things moved and the room felt different, but she was never truly into what she was totally capable of. After awhile, as I remember it, she just lay down the cards and never went back. She had a huge heart and would talk to everyone and show them what she knew; she was just pressured from those around her to stop. All that time that she did do what she knew, I was a part of it without being a part of it. I was always there just watching and learning.

I mention her now to honor her and also because this is an example of a sleeper who did not venture forth to honor her true abilities, one who I was to learn from. When the learning was through, we were both to move on. When I was younger, I started to get into astrology. My guides came right in and asked, "Are you having fun?" I would say, "This is very confusing, and I don't know what I am to do with it." They would laugh and say, "Because you are much more than that, you do not need to understand that which is not your path to follow." To this day, I do not do astrology. I do not know the birth zodiac symbology as to tell you what a Leo or Capricorn is. You can give me your birth date. I say, "Okay, but what am I to do with it?"

I come from love when I describe all of this. I honor the Sleepers, psychics, astrologers and mediums, for they chose to be here and prepare the way for those who will follow. They just forgot exactly their own missions and let the ego self come through in their lives and work, and to this they were quietly put to sleep with their gifts. It could have come from a breakdown of emotions, letting their own self-importance become an obstacle with who they truly were. As that happens, the physical body becomes not a clean and clear vehicle but a damaged and used one. All of this was too much for the ordinary person to understand and be a part of, so slowly they sat back on their own profession as a psychic or medium. Some, like I said before, kept working, but they would start telling the individual what they wanted to hear in their readings. They started doing hokey things to keep people interested in them. Some even let their ego negative side come in and blind them into an acceptance of what was going on. This happens so slowly that most were not even aware of what was happening until it was too late, and they just did not have an interest any longer. Oh, they talked a good story now and then, but nothing like they could have before. Those who stayed aware and open are your teachers of today that so many people are aware of. They are in the news, in many books and on talk shows. They have their own role to play in this spiritual evolution of opening and a huge responsibility to all those before them who are asking, "What is my spiritual journey, gifts and abilities, and how do I too learn as you?"

Sleepers did not share what their knowledge was, but the time has come for them to work with the Newbies. The Sleepers are to teach the Newbies about their own knowledge and that of the spiritual realms as Newbies are here to share their love with the Sleepers. As all of this comes together, a new day of awakening will be presented to all.

So, what did they know? Well, we are going to look more closely at this in a moment.

Chapter IV

Society's Conditioning

All of this leads into Society's Conditioning. As I say this, I want you to sit back and try to remember all of the events that placed you in society's way of thinking on every level within your being. As we are born, we are instructed in that which will make us the perfect person to be accepted by our friends, families, social groups and associates. We are taught about speech, what each item is as it is placed in our hands and what it is used for, gender identification, personality traits, which foods to eat, all about mother nature, religious structures, and the list goes on and on.

When you have children and your child is placed in your arms the first time, all sorts of emotions come into play. A rush of emotions so great there are no words. The love and promises whispered in their little ears. The beauty of this perfect little one that you helped bring onto this world, how you envision their life to be and what roles you will then play. As time goes on, you teach and love that little child. You coddle them and feed them what you know to be good for their bodies and health, you dress them just like you want and then the process begins of teaching and showing them how to be a perfect little one: how to talk and say words, what to touch and to stay away from, how to go potty, the doctor visits to learn if your child is healthy and if you are being a good parent. School comes in, and you visit to introduce your child, meet the teacher and drop off supplies, register and enroll your child into the activities you believe they would like. You take your child to church to introduce them to God and religion, and you guide them toward social contact with other children you would like them to be friends with. You help them with homework, and the list goes on and on.

All of this is what is called society's conditioning – a layering of veils. You are teaching the little one you love everything that you were taught from the one who loved and raised you, according to what was placed upon them by the society in which we live. With the exception of all the things that you want your little one to have that you did not have, you are placing that which you hold dear and close to you in the ears and eyes of your own little one.

You have a job that you go to every day – day in and day out. You see and work with the same people. Some might change, but you still develop and grow in friendships with your coworkers. As you get to know one another, there is this bell that goes off in your head that you know whom you can talk to you and whom you cannot, especially about the really important things in your life and what it all means to you. Sometimes you make the mistake of telling someone something that later comes back in your face. However, the most crucial of all of these considerations is what we do to our own self when it comes to pleasing others or trying to fit in with whatever social crowd we are involved with. We need to dress a certain way; we need to eat certain things. We need to be a part of this or that social activity, listening to these friends as they advise you, "Why would you like that person? They are so weird." "Did you see what she was wearing today?" "She does not go to our church." "My children only play with those who are in the same football league."

All of this is what is a part of that society's conditioning. We let society dictate to us on every level each day. We allow it because we do not want to stand out in the crowd or for others to make fun of us. We don't want to be rejected from their social graces, and then we in turn become just like those around us. This, then, is transferred to our children, and the cycle keeps spinning from one generation to the next.

That's the layering of veils. As each one of these veils is placed upon us as we grow from child to young adult to adult, it is like the recognizable onion with many layers to peel away to discover who we really are. This is exactly what happens as we have a spiritual awakening; we start to learn. As we learn, we start to peel back the layers of the veils. You know these veils. They are all of the ones you hear so much about: the veils of concealment, the veils with spirit, which everyone works so hard to see through. What no one has told you, though, is that this is the layering of society's conditioning, the issues and resentments that have been placed upon us that we have absorbed and accepted as our own; this then creates and forms into larger issues and resentments. As we grow and learn in our awakening process, we start to peel back the layers of years and years of issues and resentments so that the veils become transparent. Spirit becomes so much clearer to see, hear, sense, smell, taste and know.

How many times have you said to yourself, "I wish I could see as others see?" Well, yes, you can, but first you must sit down and do the work that will assist you in removing these veils. Building your foundation can be intimidating at first since you will be tearing down that construct of your life that has been an important part of you for so long. I will be the first to say that it is not easy, but it is so worth the endeavor to take you further in this life than you have ever gone before. With this spiritual evolution, you will come across so many people who are having this epiphany that they are here for bigger things or there has to be something more to all of this.

Years ago, I sat and listened to my guides as they told me that the prayers of the world are being answered. No one had taken the time to truly look around them before, but this was changing. More people were beginning to become aware of how it is so easy to rely on negativity. It does not change and is easy to be a part of, but those who choose to step up and make the conscious choice to change and work with the light of God find a greater whole. Energies have shifted to a giving – not a wanting. The children being born the past 10 to 20 years are here to place themselves in this from start to finish. They are the ones who sat and heard our prayers and would ask God, "Is it time yet?" Then the day came when they asked, and God said, "Yes." These children are here for you and me. We are here as forerunners, clearing the way and getting people used to the ideas; the children will be the ones implementing them. Look around you in society and watch what is offered for our children right now in the way of cartoons. There is a whole host of them, teaching our children about spirit, guides and powers that they have. It is very easy to see that they are to be kept aware of who they are with all of these and more. Even more TV shows are coming out with those who have gifts and powers; it is so incredible that society is slowly being reconditioned to accept that which has been here from the very beginning. It is up to the individual to finally build their own foundation to be a part of that change.

Some of us are even taught at a very tender age about abuse, whether substance, mental or physical. It is all the same – abuse. We cannot see it for what it is because we are taught that it is the correct way of life. Do you think a child of an abusive home has any say about what is going on? That is why the next time you see that child who does not quite fit in with any of their own peers, a child being ridiculed for being quiet, weird, not dressed the best, send them love and acceptance because you do not know that which is going on in their life.

Social conditioning has been going on before our own time; it goes back to the very first books ever cut out in stone and masonry. It is the social conditioning of what we are taught to accept in our lives, how to think, act and be. But now we are beginning to see the reality: when we start to live as others tell us to live and be what others tell us to be, that is not for the greater good but for the lower ego. As we grow in this awareness, we evolve and recognize that which we do not want to pass onto our children so we may ensure that they will not be held back from all that there is for them to reach out and be!

Chapter V

The Visionary "Eyes Wide Open"

As a visionary, my life is filled each day and night with that which is given to me by spirit, meaning those who are deceased, our guides, angels, teachers and loved ones in the spirit realms. This relates to all things visual that I can see right in front of me with my eyes wide open or in my mind's eye, which you know to be the "third eye." This makes life very interesting. When I say "third eye," it means I am looking at something with my eyes open or closed. Images appear in my mind to show me what I need to know. It is like having a movie screen running in front of you holographically inside your head. These images appear from energies and those in spirit who show us what we need to know or see to assist and guide us. If I see a picture, I will automatically receive a knowing of that person and the events that they have gone through in their life, what the personality is or was like and a few other things that my guides are trying to tell me is important. Now there are times that not a lot comes from the picture that is given to me, and they will then tell me why.

Much of what I see with my "eyes wide open" may come in the form of specific pictures, apparitions or visual frames that I must decipher. These are called signs and symbols. These symbols make up the whole of the way those in spirit will communicate with you, much as putting a puzzle together. I must have all of the pieces – symbols – and then I can begin to lay it out and piece it together in my mind's eye. As I do so, those in spirit will give me feelings/sensations, words (audible and written out in my mind's eye) to assist me in understanding what they are showing me, to understand the message as a whole to give to others or for my own understanding. It is in learning and developing all of this that I then teach to others with the guidance and assistance from those in the spiritual realms.

So it is working with that which you think is different or unusual in your life that makes you who you are this day. As a child, I, like you, believed that what I saw in front of me was the truth. This is a correct view of life with everyone. I see someone standing here talking and showing me something and so, then, do you. On the playground in school, with my "eyes wide open" I would physically see an angel or person standing beside another playmate. When I asked them about who the person was and why they were ignoring them, the other kids would laugh or say I was weird because no one was there and they would run away. This was crucial in my understanding of myself and what was going on. It did not stop me, but it did make me go inside and seek counsel with myself. I learned not speak of it to my playmates but to listen to what the other person in spirit was saying and then try to help them anyway I could. Sometimes this was disastrous, and sometimes it all worked out. I was learning. As those in spirit would visit me to teach me things, we would sit in my grandmother's backyard under the trees and have what we call play school. I would sometimes be the pupil and at other times I was the teacher. I was honored enough to meet my grandfather (who had just transitioned), the angels, fairies, deva's, my family members, those seeking assistance (earth bounds).

Then I met The Blessed Mother. She was like a queen who glowed so bright that I was in love with her from the moment I saw her. She is beautiful, wise, kind and loving, and always has something to say about children. She would visit and tell me what I was learning and why. She always told me, "There will be a time in your life when I will call you and others to assist me." She asked me, "Will you be ready, child of my heart?" I would laugh and say, "I am ready right now, Mother." She lovingly would say, "Soon enough." As the years went on, I would cry and ask to go home as I could not take that which was going on in this life. The same would always be told to me, "Soon enough. I bring you all the love from the Divine and know that you truly are the Divine."

I learned how to know what the trees and Mother Earth were saying, how to listen to them and understand what was given to me. I experienced traveling the world and viewing what I needed to see for the betterment of the human race. I was learning to a different degree all that I needed to keep me aware of who I was and to trust who I was. This developed over my whole childhood and made for quite an interesting exposure of the best and worst of human living that we go through. I, like you, needed to experience what it is like to be a physical person living a physical existence, even knowing I was a spiritual aspect of God. I was of this world, but I am of no world to which we know.

It is working with that which you think is different or unusual in your life that makes you who you are this day. We have an understanding that we want something more or different in our lives. We have this gut feeling that we need to do or learn about things that no one really wants to talk about or knows about. So what do we do? We go to the local bookstore and start looking for books that will give us the answers, or we Google our way through the Internet. We spend hours pouring through one and then another and start to see a correlation between that which we are feeling and that which we are seeking, but still there is nothing there that gives us all the answers. We start to *gather*; we gather all that there is and start to read, devouring the words that bring it all together. We join groups, classes and workshops of learning. Once again, we are taking pieces of the puzzle to lay them out and to start placing them together to make the whole picture because within this whole picture we will find ourselves.

So I ask you, who are you right now in this moment of time? Me? I am a visionary messenger. I work with all the "Clair's" in everything I do, so much that it is now just a part of me, I do not feel a difference in my life. Sometimes my children will say, "we want to just talk to you without you doing that stuff", I have to laugh as I say to them "that stuff is as much a part of me as I am of it". However, I will then try to just be and listen to what they are saying as I know what they are really asking for is just to have someone to listen to them as they think aloud. I still receive so much information; I just learn to be still and quiet. After awhile, they will then say "Okay just tell me what you got" which then starts me laughing all over again.

I receive pieces each and every day and night about people, places, times, things and events; and I start to piece them together. What I see, hear, feel, sense and know can make your head spin and does mine, sometimes. I see events in your life that have already happened and that will happen. I see tragedies and celebrations. I see love and disasters. Some things that, I enjoy and wish you well. Some things I do not care to see, but it is a message for me to know and then I need to know what to do with it. Those are the times when I find myself standing there saying, "Now, what did I need to know that for?" and having the sensation of whether it is critical to know right now or will actually take place later.

Chapter VI

Psychometry

As a visionary, when I pick something up, I will go back in time to see just about everything that is associated with the object and those who have touched it. The thing that I need to do is to focus, as there can be many individuals who have touched upon it. I will need to understand all of what I am seeing, feeling, sensing, hearing, smelling and knowing to get to the time period that it is connected with. This is sometimes easy and sometimes very frustrating as there are those who want an answer right away; they do not understand the layers that I go through to get what is needed and can take a few minutes.

This is called Psychometry, a form of extrasensory perception wherein a psychic, medium or visionary holds an object in his or her hands in order to obtain information about the object or its owner. Extrasensory perception, or ESP, is defined in parapsychology as the ability to acquire information by means such as telepathy, clairvoyance and precognition other than the five main senses of taste, sight, touch, smell and hearing. The term implies sources of information currently unknown to science. Extrasensory perception is also sometimes referred to as a **sixth sense**

This is sometimes very tricky, as the images I receive will also be fragmented like puzzles pieces that I have to decipher and piece together, which is a big part of why it takes a few moments to get it right. With these objects, I will also be able to see future happenings – precognition – that will transpire for people, places, things and events. When this happens, I go through many emotions as it relates to the individual or place. This is a very serious responsibility, for you then have within you something that can change a person's life, or that can affect whole families, businesses, countries and so much more. You need to be able to look at the whole picture before you blurt it out to the one asking, and to understand what is for the greater good. If I am being shown or told something, it is not always necessary for the recipient to hear it. It is necessary for me to have a better understanding of the recipient so that I can then assist them in getting to where they need to be; this is where the huge responsibility comes in. I will sit in class and give future predictions, which I love to do; but there is a fine line in wanting these events to take place (for confirmation of your message/prediction) and wanting to see a change so that which you see will never happen.

As someone who does this for a living, what you need to consider is whether you live with that message or prediction you have given. *For even though it may not seem to affect you at that moment of time, it will; it is then to be revealed as to when it does affect you.* For if you have affected another's life, it may then come back to affect you later in your life! I am deeply committed to everyone understanding their responsibility to another living being in this world on all levels. I can take just about anything you give me and look at it, and sure enough a picture will appear which turns into a story or prediction. When you look around you, what do you see with your "eyes wide open?"

Chapter VII

Truth Indicator

Seeing with "eyes wide open" is a wonderful way to live your life; it can also be the worst way to live life. When I was younger, I would see so much and just blurt out what I saw and then pay the price for doing so. My younger years were filled with much confusion when it came to this. Like other clairvoyant individuals in this world, I too have so many stories to tell: good and not good. It was not easy seeing earthbound spirits around someone or in their homes, businesses, vehicles, yard, bike, etc., and talk to them and try to understand why the person with me would not be talking to them. I would have conversations and then the person with me would say, "stop that," or "What are you doing – weirdo," "stop scaring me," all the way to "stop embarrassing me" and "stop that lying." It was amazing to see beautiful angels with someone and having them say, "Oh how nice, but you know angels are not real so stop telling stories." I would look at the angels, and they would smile and stay with them anyway. I guess one of the hardest things for me to tell people was about the gifts I have in seeing a person for who they really are.

When I look at someone, I can see his or her spirit or soul. This is in a way my truth indicator when meeting someone or talking with a person. As we are talking, or I am looking at them converse or stand there, I can see what is called a 3-D holographic image over the person's face. In class, we call this morphing: to morph one image into another through a seamless transition of time and space. As this happens, the reality of who this individual is then is made known to me and is seen up close, front and center. Now this has been happening to me since the age of four, but as I got older and went through everyone telling me how strange or weird I was, I would never tell anyone about what I was seeing again. As a child, we all have ridden in the car with our parents looking out the windows at the scenery as we ride along. As a car or vehicle would drive by us, I would look at the person in the vehicle beside us. All of a sudden, they would change from what my physical perception of them was. I would see a woman who would be glowing a beautiful yellow color, like the sun shining so bright, and I could see her soul star look over to me and smile. At that moment, I would hear the heavenly angelic choirs singing in glory so crystal clear that I would then start to sing with them. At other times, the individual riding up next to us would be dark in appearance, like a heavy smoke cloud was around them. Then their soul star would look over at me with the ugliest of faces, and I could feel the terror of their soul to the deepest of levels. I would always shrink back, so they would not notice me anymore, as I felt they could jump right out and come after me. This would happen so much that after awhile I started to identify and remember what went on during these exchanges and piece the symbols together, like having my own memory file that I would then pull up to understand the relations to the different colors, pictures and sensations I was feeling. I came to see that when an individual was holding any motive that was not from the light, their "ugly side comes out." This is a huge symbol, for me to know just what they are all about and that their soul star is one that is not good. On the other hand, when an individual is from the light and has such a wonderful soul, I see this light so bright come from them and their faces that it is like nothing will hold it back. I love being around them. Even if this individual is going through hard times, their soul star shines out for me to see.

As I grew into my teen years, I tried not to validate what I saw as I turned away from what was being shown to me. I just wanted to have good friends and be like them. Funny how we want that which is not the best for us and do not realize it until we go through something that gets us back on track.

Around the age of nineteen, I was sitting with a girlfriend at the local pizza place trying to figure why I was having a hard time with another friend. As I was talking to my girlfriend about it, I looked at her and her face morphed right into a pig face. I stopped talking; I could hardly believe how ugly and horrible looking it was. At first I was not fazed, and then it stayed that way. As she kept talking, I went into myself and asked my guardian angel, "What is it I am supposed to know about this friend?" My guardian angel immediately showed me how this girlfriend had been spreading rumors that were not true about me to a whole group of friends and their parents because she was jealous of me. I sat there with my mouth open, looking at my girlfriend who still had this pig face, and then other things came out to show itself to me with a huge darkness that surrounded her. I had had enough and told her goodbye and left, so you understand she was my friend no more. To this day, I can still see this so clearly when I think of her. After that time I started working once again more closely with these gifts and would start to research the many files in my memory.

"These are the times in which you find yourself standing there and saying, "Now, what did I need to know that for," and then the sensation of whether it is critical to know right now or will actually take place later." Adele

Chapter VIII

Death and Transitioning, How I See It

Now, I will make it clear that, yes, I see death. I will see it for an individual, event or place, and it is my responsibility to decide whether to deliver the message or not. Why would I be shown death and not say it? Well, if I told you that your loved one will be transitioning in three months, you would then anguish over what to do with that information. When you do decide to tell them, you at that moment of time have taken it upon yourself to control that individual's destiny/fate, their choice of their own life. From what happens at that moment, you will then have a responsibility over what that individual does with their life. Make sense? Oh yes, you will watch them either get angry and use denial, grow depressed with that knowledge or then go to the extreme of doing everything they believe they need to do – since their life is ending. Now, what if during this time through you and their own actions that they have altered their destiny/fate with your choice of telling them they will transition in three months? What if this then will be sooner or later? What if you have played such a huge role that this brings none of it about? You then would be the one that this individual would come back to say a number of things, one in which would be, "You ruined my life. Why did you tell me something that never happened? Now look at this mess you got me into." Oh yes, you did this; you took the fate/destiny of another through your own responsibility and decided what they needed to know and what they did not. What of those who will come back and say, "Why did you not tell me that my mother would be dying?" To you I say, "It is not my message to deliver." After a few moments, they will see this and understand. It is so hard during these times. As I said, it is my own responsibility as to the direction of the message.

My husband will occasionally ask me, "Do you see so and so dying?" I always laugh and tell him, "For one – I do not look for it in anyone as that is a waste of my time, and then

I would be obsessed with death, which I am not; and two, I do not see it, for it is not for me to see, for then what would you do with the information?" He usually quiets down and starts to think, and then he changes the subject. He has learned in all of these years that you can try – you just might not like to know the answer.

Still, I need to mention that when I look at an individual, part of what I may see is death. I do not care for that word but know of none other to use. You see, when I look at someone and they turn a pasty white, I know they will be transitioning within three days. As I see this, I am also being shown an assortment of other things, and not everyone will be the same. Can this death be prevented? Yes and no. My daughter's girlfriend was visiting me one day with her newborn child. After a lovely visit, she was wrapping her child in blankets and hat when I looked over and the child had gone stone white. At that moment I saw him lying in a coffin and could feel the sadness all around him and his loved ones. Then his guardian angel told me to tell her to pick the child up. I immediately said, "Pick your child up and hold him and place your hands on his back as if you were burping him." All of a sudden, the child started choking. We could see something was terribly wrong, and he couldn't breathe. She picked him up and started thumping him on his back and a huge gush of formula came out. She helped him to get settled and quieted down; after a few moments, she once again laid him in his carrier to leave. I was saying goodbye again. As I looked at him, he went stone white again. I told her to pick him up again. She just stood there at first, and then I went and grabbed him out of the carrier and held him close to me. I asked God to please assist this child of his heart for his highest and best, and then he started choking again. I placed him close and turned him upside down as I worked on his back and front chest. Once again, formula came rushing out; and we cleaned him all up and settled him down. I returned him to his mother and had them stay a little while longer. When I was given the okay by his guardian angel, I let them leave. Today, he is the cutest and happiest of little boys as this one turned out for all of us to be a happy one.

Not all of them do, however. I was attending a funeral viewing for a girlfriend's family member. As we walked around and connected with those in attendance, I ran into a woman I knew from a few years past. I always have liked her, and she is a very gentle soul. She had some major problems in her life, but it was good to see her and find out how she was doing. As we were talking, she turned a pasty stone white. I looked and listened but nothing was said to me. I was only shown that there was an ending coming. After awhile, we parted ways. I knew in my heart I would never talk to her again. Later the next day, I found out she had been killed that night. She accepted a ride home from someone, and they were involved in a head-on accident. The other person survived, and this woman did not. Now, to all who knew her, she was accepted for who she was. Everyone knew she walked everywhere; she very seldom rode in a car. That night she had chosen to accept a ride; as I look back, I see her soul accepted her final choice in life to ride out in style.

Another way I see death is through visions that my loved ones in spirit give me. This is through deep sleep, which you would say to be dream time. During this time, my loved ones will come to me and show themselves as deceased in such a way that I know they are deceased and acknowledge that to them. They will then proceed to show me through a series of visions of symbology and stories that will relate to the physical loved one in my life who will be transitioning and in such detail as to let me know how I will be involved with them as they transition. This has been going on since I was a very young girl. By now, my knowledge of the visions has grown so strong there are no doubts as to the message. When my loved ones in spirit come to me like this, there is nothing that will change the outcome. It is written, and they are making me aware of it so that I might be prepared and assist the individual or others around who will be involved. Helping them to understand when the time comes is one of the hardest things for me to do because most individuals and family members do not know what to think of me and who I am. It is very humbling to know you have been given this gift of knowing what is about to take place and to be a part of something so beautiful as a welcoming home and the loneliness as it all unfolds. You are left with a huge hole in your heart from the one who will no longer be a part of your physical life that you loved so much, and, on top of it all, the words that are spoken from your loved one still here in the physical as they go through the mourning process. As I said before, this is a gift, one that you must have faith in your heart to know you are loved like no other can give you here in this physical life, for you will be alone in this work to some degree. This gift is also rewarding to the fullest of senses, and it's one that I would not choose to miss by any means.

When my own mother transitioned on November 22, 2005, it was devastating. I am the only daughter in a family of seven children, and I loved my mom dearly. As with any large family, you have the relationship you have; no one knows it as you yourself. Just as I do not know the full relationship my mother has with each one of her sons, they do not know our relationship we have together. We know what we hear, but then what are the real truths? Of course, my family is not fully supportive of what and who I am, but my mother was supportive in her own way. She so loved the angels and the children. In May of 2005, my husband and I went to the beach to get away for a weekend. Each one of the nights we were away, my loved ones in spirit came to see me, each time with a message of death. Now, it was up to me to understand what they showed me, and it was clear. Mom was going to transition, and it would be before Christmas that year. I did not know what to do at first; Mom did not say anything was wrong. I could not just go up and say, "Granddaddy came to see me, and he said you would be joining him soon." I waited to see what else was going to go on. The next month, the other message played out and my husband's uncle passed away. My guides had told me that last Christmas, that he would not see the next. As my loved ones came to me in my vision, they confirmed it; then he gently made his choice to go home.

As I was waiting for information regarding Mom, she and Dad came by the house one day. As my mother was sitting on my couch, I looked at her. In her place, I saw her mother, my grandmother, sitting there and looking at me. She looked just like I remember her ? so tiny and quiet, just watching. She told me everything was going to be fine, and she was with Mom every day. There was nothing I could do, and I needed to just be there for my mother. Mom did not talk about her illness; she did not want to bother anyone. She took this one on herself and was going to hold it for as long as she could. I then went with my mother to the oncologist. You see, my mother was a five-year breast cancer survivor. She was going on six years, and the cancer had gone to her liver. That day, she was a pale yellow as we went into the room where they give you your chemo treatment. She sat in the chair, and the doctor came in to say no, not today; I need to talk to you. We went into her office, and she point-blank said, "I will be sending hospice to your home. Please make her as comfortable as possible." Even though I knew this moment was coming, I could not do or say anything. I looked at Mom, and she just smiled and looked into my eyes. Even though she did not speak one word to me, she said a lifetime of words at that moment. It was so surreal we both knew what Hospice meant we both just looked at each other. No words were spoken neither one of us could of said anything, instead as we looked at one another. We saw so many years pass us by, so many words that were spoken and unspoken, so many things that needed to be done and un-done. We both said "I love you," as we waited for my dad to finish talking to the doctor. As he came back in the room to take us home, my Mom stood straight and proud. She held her head up as she walked back through the chemo room, passing by everyone who knew the news she just received. I was so proud of her as we walked out that door.

Those next two weeks went by in a whirlwind of activity. Watching everyone walking around numb from the news, coming by to say hello, talking about everything from memories of moments in time to whose birthday is when and how old they are. Being beside my mother was the most precious of times for me; sharing in this was a painful experience but one that I treasure. Helping my father go through doing what was needed from the individuals who came by from hospice to family members understanding what was going on. I took no joy from what was going on, but I knew, as many of you do, that I was there to assist my parents in anyway I could and be the one who I prayed could help hold the glue together for everyone. If anyone freaked out, then so too would others and then a family explosion would have taken place. Dad was in no condition to go through all of this by himself, as if we would have let him. Everything from those moments on were for Mom and all of what she taught us to be in who we are.

As a visionary, the most awesome sight for me to see, as I always do when someone is in this stage of their transition, is watching those in spirit arrange and orchestrate every single part of the experience. You see, our loved ones, guides, angels, teachers and other assistants are there every step of the way. They orchestrate the whole process. We may think we are making certain decisions by being where we need to be, staying around the area of the home or hospital, dropping by and helping the family out in any way, getting time off work to visit, cook food, whatever the case may be. All the way to how long we stay for that visit to which area we are in when the time of transition is going on. I am here to tell you that it is this wonderful loving army of individuals in spirit, who are calling all the shots. They do so as part of our contract we made before being born here on Mother Earth. From the one in spirit I call the general, an individual who has the clipboard of the events unfolding, to the angels, family members in spirit, our guides you have with you, to ascended masters, everyone is working together to make all of it a beautiful and easy experience both for our loved one who is transitioning and for us.

My mom never did talk to anyone about what was coming and how she felt. She did not want others to feel bad or to hold onto the burden of what she was going though. She was a spiritual person who loved her angels. She was not afraid of this process of transitioning, for she knew that she would be in the arms of God and she was going home. As we all gathered around her, Mom transitioned quietly on that November day. At her side was the Blessed Mother Mary and all of Moms family members who are in spirit, ones who I had not seen since I was a little girl and had gone to their funerals. All of this comes crashing back, and feeling their love once again embrace my mother was very tender and beautiful. I knew in my heart of hearts that what I have always been given was cemented in stone that night as the Blessed Mother had promised to me from the very beginning: *"I will always be with you and yours."*

With all of this, the whole thing came about just as I was shown all those months earlier in my series of visions, all the way down to the very last detail of those who would be in the room physically with her as she transitioned. I would have not wanted this for anything, to lose the one who brought me into this life, to lose the mother that is always there when I needed her the most, but I have to honor my mother with all of it. I had to honor the contract that we had together, to be by her side during this time. She was a beautiful and strong woman who brought seven children into this world. She guided us to be who we are to this day. As I look back on so many memories, I see where my mother was my physical guide here on Mother Earth to assist me to always walk in the light of God, to be who I am here to be and do the work I am here to do.

So as this can be a blessing to some, it is also one that I accept with the huge responsibility of knowing when I am to deliver a message or not. It is the same for you. All those in spirit will guide you, for what you receive will be from divine guidance. It is up to you to be aware of what to do with the message. Your divine guidance will always point you in the direction of the highest and greatest good because God is the source of the highest vibration of all those in spirit who work with you for all the reasons of his source. As this is said, the highest of divine guidance of all from God – is.

"Unconditional Love. Love yourself enough to know the direction in which you go with this work and have it always be around that of Love." Adele

So yes, I do see death, but I will also be shown if it is for me to say that which is being shown to me, or keep it and advise the person who is the subject of what I have seen in a way that may assist and guide that person into another scenario, so that the outcome may be different. There are times that I will flat-out say what is being shown to me. These times I will tell the individual, one whom I have known for a period of time, and that individual will know their degree of responsibility. If I am being pushed from my guides, then I must say it as it is a matter of more than life and death. On the other hand, can we not change that which is called destiny/fate? Yes, you betcha! At the time that I see what is given to me by spirit, it is the absolute truth – in that moment of time.

"As time is irrelevant, then so too is the outcome in many situations and so is not to be discounted lightly."

Chapter IX

Understanding and Responsibility

*Y*our *Guides, Angels, Teachers and Loved Ones in Spirit as they reach out to work with you.*

Before we go any further, I would like to tell you about my counsel of Angelic Wise Ones. They play the biggest role in my life on so many levels, and you will need to know them as we go along. As with each of you, I have a counsel of guides and teachers who are in the spiritual realms. These are individuals who have had previous lifetimes in this physical world. They have chosen to be my "Counsel of One" to guide, assist, nurture, protect, advise, teach, make me aware of, love, etc., to connect with on all levels of my own life right here and now through their own wisdom, knowledge, understanding, experience, love, sense of humor, abilities, compassion, peace and so much more of who they were in each of their own lifetimes and that which they are now for me. Each of my guides and teachers in my Counsel are my best friends; they know me more than anyone here in this physical life. They do not lie to me, they are not mean to me and they do not tell me negative things. That is not in them, for what do they have to gain in doing so? Nothing! Like me, they are learning that which they need to know in order for their own ascension in their realms. As they guide me, I am working with them to guide them also, for that which they also need for their own growth. We are a team of teaching and learning, and that is a very powerful thing.

When I am opened to receiving their guidance, they have the utmost love for me and those with whom I am working. When they show or tell me something, it is either for me or the individual to have an understanding of what is going on or what is going to go on; and it comes from the purest of love. Are they connected to the God Source? You betcha, as we all are. We are divided aspects of God. It is for us to discover and remember each of those aspects as we grow in this life of learning and understanding that we are here to reconnect with the Love of God. In doing so, we are gathering those puzzle pieces, laying them out and connecting them to make a whole. When we have reached the whole of who we are, we will have peace and the knowing of who we are and the Love of God that is with us. Then and only then will we have Peace here on Earth. Can you imagine what that would look like on a whole of the human evolution here at this time? Amazing!

I need to mention my angels as they are a part of my Counsel. The angels have not had an incarnated life here on Mother Earth. I just could not place them with the guides and teachers in my explanations, as this would have made you raise too many conflicting questions; I bring them here to you now. When I was very young, my deceased grandfather had introduced my angels to me in such a loving way that I never questioned their work with me. I call them my "Angelic Wise Ones" and over the years have incorporated my guides and teachers in this class also. For the angels are true messengers of God – he sends them to all of us in our time of need and when we ask for their assistance. I do not worship them, nor would they allow me to do so, as they are in constant praise to God. When we do ask them for assistance and guidance, it is through the voice, energy and power of God that they are then with us. When we bow our heads in prayer to God, he then sends his loving angels to be with us. In knowing this, we know that God is among us and loves us dearly. My angels, as well as yours, truly love us unconditionally and will always be there to work, protect, guide, teach, communicate and love us in every aspect of our lives; we just need to ask.

So with each of my angels, guides and teachers in my counsel, I have gotten to know them and work with them on a daily basis. I know what they look like and how their energies feel. I can tell the difference between them just as you can tell the difference in all of your friends, as each of them are a unique aspect of the energy you associate with them. We do have freedom of choice in our lives, a "free will of choice" as most people like to say. I use my free will of choice to listen to my guides and teachers and trust them so much that whatever they tell me I follow, as they guide me though all I need. Now, this is not to be confused with the experience of someone telling you that "a spirit cannot tell you what to do" because they are right. My guides can tell me what to do all they want; it is up to me to decide what to do. It is then my responsibility to do what I know and what I have been taught to do – the right thing! How do I know it is right? They have taught me to be one with God, and God always shows me the right thing to do!

Even though I have been blessed to be "open" from the time of my birth to be connected to spirit, I want you to understand this has not always been a blessing, as you would think. As I said before, I was still connected strongly to my spirit-form after I was born here on earth. In the physical, I was experiencing things that no one else was. I did not know the difference. I believed you and I were the same, and we could do and see the same. *As you see a child, try to go to their level of awareness; you will be amazed at what you really do find.* I did not find out differently until I would talk about the person standing in the doorway that no one else was seeing or that I was flying outside my grandparents' home visiting other family members at their homes. I knew everything that was going on in their home. Even though I was not physically in their home, I knew what they really thought of me though they had not said it directly to me. Since I could hear them say it, I would then tell them what I thought of them. Then, of course, they would cry and go home; I was the mean one. I would then be so hurt because why was I at fault if they said it first? Can you see how that would make this life challenging? Finally, just laying in your bed and crying because you did not want to be here anymore. It was not what you thought it would be, and there was no way you were going to make it to do what you came for, and why could I not just be the age I needed to be to do my work?

At a very tender age, you learn how to lie; what a horrid way to have to live. If you told the truth about what was going on, you were called a liar and an embarrassment. You had to learn not to tell the truth in order for those around you to like you and not get mad at you. Isn't life inflexible enough without having to go through this? You learn how to adapt and live with who you are. You try then to make friendships and have relationships. The whole time you know so much in the truth, but you cannot live it for then no one will like having you around.

Once I was at a party with some friends, and a group of people came in that no one really knew. As everyone was asking questions about them, I just started talking and telling everyone about who they were. I had never met them before, but I knew them. My guides and angels came in and gave me all I wanted. When I was done and the others found out what I said was true, they all turned and said how weird I was, what I freak I was. I was never more embarrassed before in my life. As a teenager, it was hard enough going through those years and harder yet when you had to be something that you were not for others to accept or like you. What I finally did find in those years is that I did not have to do the things I thought would make me friends; I needed to do what was right so that I could be my own friend and be who I AM.

As you see, you are normal and right in how you feel and who you are. You do not need to change yourself and seek out that which you believe society says who you need to be or have friends. I have the greatest group of friends right now, and I am truly happy, healthy and normal. I have learned through all of this I am who I am, and I will not live who I am not.

When we work with our Counsel, we will be feeling their energies. When you are thinking of your loved one, a warming sensation comes over you. You have a large smile, and you go back in time to that moment of happiness, seeing them as they were, hearing their laughter. Some feel it as a cooling sensation over their bodies. When my guides stand around me, each of them has their own resonance of energies that distinguishes them from the other. My joy guide is light and airy and will usually come in around my knees or shoulders or whirls around the top of my head. My protector guide comes in with a strength of warmth and compassion. I can feel him standing to the side of me as if you are in a grocery store and someone stands beside you in line. The amount of energy will be in who is there. If you feel something light and airy and then turn, you may see a child or young lady. If the energy is stronger, it may be that of a male or even two. Take the time, close your eyes and feel all that is around you. This is one of the easiest ways to know who is near. Next time when you are with your family or friends, stand next to someone and close yourself off to everyone and just feel. Feel how you are reacting to their presence. Does it feel good, warm, special, harmful, uneasy, excited, etc.? Then open yourself back to those around you and laugh when you guess the right one.

I have a series of meditation CDs that will introduce you to one of your many guides, angels and teachers in spirit.

These CDs are identical to the meditations I use in my classes to assist my students in meeting those in spirit. It is a wonderful tool, one that lets you begin your journey of connection as it opens you to a whole new level.

What is the most important aspect of our work with those in the spiritual and physical realms? It is our responsibility. As you have read many times, it is our one saving grace in who we are. We must be responsible for all that comes from our own mouths. We have those who have a need of an understanding to what is happening in their lives, what they can do, where they can go and what is the meaning of all of it. If we are not careful, the ego can come in and twist our own around. When I work with someone, they have my undivided attention. It is not up to me to tell them what is going on unless they can first say it themselves, and then that opens the doors for me to assist them.

If we are responsible in clearing and cleansing ourselves on a daily basis, clearing and cleansing our homes on a daily basis, saying our prayers with protection and invocation, inviting God and the angelic realms to be with you, staying grounded, keeping out of other's business or gossiping, keeping our hearts open to the Love that is given to us, then those who will be before us will be the recipient of that love too. To journal from our hearts in the truest of honesty.

This I call being a clear and clean vehicle, one that is focused and disciplined in who and what they are. They work with themselves each day in the above areas and more, to be the cleanest conduit of energy they can be, to then give to you on any level. I know that if you go to a medium, psychic or healer and they have so many issues and resentments and plain old problems in their own life, then that energy will be transferred to you as the recipient of the energy that they will work with in the reading, guidance or healing you are receiving. I ask you, when was the last time you thought about the energy a person is bringing in through their own lives that you then let them work with and on you? If you are in front of a professional individual who is going to give you mediumship messages, a healing session or psychic reading, and they did not feel right to you, what will you do then? Stay and let them work with you, or gently excuse yourself and leave? This is what I say as "we learn by trial and error." If I meet someone and their energy is not right, if I know they have problems that they are not addressing, I will not go through with any appointment I may have with them until they decide to do their own work and become a clean conduit once again.

If you are seeking to work with those in the spiritual realms, you need to be clear in what direction in which to work. You need to learn and work with your foundation and then build upon that. Gather everything you can in all areas of that field, know yourself inside and out, have a belief and faith structure that will not fall in around you. Look at your strengths and weaknesses, deal with your resentments and issues, take a long, close look honestly at yourself and do your work. Do your journaling and most importantly meditate, even if it is fifteen minutes a day!

Be patient; it will all come as it is meant to be.

So many times I have seen those who come in and are newly awakened, and then they want to go right into teaching others. This is a great intention, but they have not learned what is being taught to them. They need to build their foundation (this I cannot say enough), for this is what will keep them in the light of who they are, an understanding of all things. If there is no understanding in their own foundation, they are skipping vital information about what they need to keep going on their paths.

If you have a very good teacher, the teacher will encourage you and teach you that which you need to be strong and move into your place in the world. A spiritual teacher is not one who wants their students to stay with them as a student for life. A spiritual teacher is one who will guide you, to empower you to be who you are meant to be and move you to do that which you are here to do. Most spiritual teachers will tell you it took them years to be the teacher they are right now; they went through a learning period of hard work and discipline to do so. If your foundation is weak, then you will fall. This is not easy for me to say but it is a truth that has been shown to me over and over again.

These next steps are the building of your foundation:

Love

Honesty

Prayer

Journaling

Meditation

Cleansing & Clearing

Patience

Laughter

Stop right now and think back on the past year of your life. What have you accomplished? How long did it take for that year to go by? Wasn't it just yesterday that ....When you look back on this past year of your life, you will see how quickly it all actually went, how much was or wasn't accomplished. If that year went by that fast, just think of how fast it will go by now with you having these tools to assist you along the way. It is only what you make it to be. For me, the past twenty some years or so went by so fast, once I decided to live my truths. I honor you for starting to live yours now!

Now let's get to work. This book is also about what you are experiencing right now and how you can help yourself be who you are! Be forewarned. I will be tweaking you in this journey as I do all of my students, but it will be from the highest of love that I have for you to assist and guide you where you need to be in this lifetime right now. We have all opened the doors of knowledge at the highest level of the Godhead, and there is no backing away from that which you are here to learn and who you are to be. There is a calling at this time for all of the forerunners to step out and to teach those who are calling for the light to surround them to bring all of us on a global level together for peace. For when there is Peace on this Earth with every living thing, then we all shall have Heaven Here on Earth!!!

"In all things you will start to see: we are all divided aspects of God and that in each of us is an aspect of another, until you take all of these pieces and place them together; then you have a whole in which it is the whole of God." Blessings,"
Adele

Chapter X

Building Your Foundation

If you have picked up this book and proceeded this far, then: 1) your angels and guides have brought it to your attention for a reason, and you are a little open to the spiritual aspect of learning who you are and why you are here right now; or 2) you have been on this journey and still there is something missing that you are seeking. So to all of you I say, "Welcome. You have chosen to be awakened in the purest of Light of God's love. Let us begin the journey of your lifetime together."

When we first start to develop or awaken, we start searching for what we need. We start to gather the information that we can get our teeth into for an understanding. This is building our basic foundation, and it is one of the most important aspects in all of our journey, in our progress and ascension. Without this foundation, the construct of who we believe ourselves to be will eventually fall in around us.

As I mentioned at the start of this book, whether you want to develop yourself to be a psychic, medium, visionary, minister, channel, angel reader, psychic detective, healer, a better person, etc., you need the basic knowledge to stand on. In this chapter, we will look at just what it is you need.

A journal is the most essential piece of knowledge that you can have. If you do not have one, please take the time to go and find one that you will be using just for this work. It does not have to be anything fancy, just one to call your own.

A religious background is not needed, but a religious understanding is one that helps build the bottom of the foundation. All of it is centered on the God in all of us. The relationship you have with God is the root of your foundation.

Do you have a feeling inside that you are expecting something great to happen?

- Is there something you feel is missing in your life?
- Where do you stand with God right now?
- How does all of this feel in your gut when it comes to your religious faith and understanding?
- Does it clash with it, or can it stand on its own?
- Do you believe in reincarnation, and what if you do not?
- What do you really believe you need to know about religion to go any further?

Take a few moments, be honest with yourself and answer the above questions. When I say honest, I believe you are being honest, but are you? You see, we need to understand the level of honesty we will be using when we do this work. You can be totally honest with yourself, or you can do as you always do and tell just a smidgen of honesty to get by with. But then I will say, you are on these pages to build your basic foundation. In doing so, if you cannot be totally honest, then you cannot build even the basic foundation. Take your time, and think about these questions. How does your gut feel as you ask the questions to yourself?

Journaling and meditation are the vital keys in all of the work we do. If you have never meditated, no problem. If you have been journaling for just a short while or for a long time, great! I will talk about meditation more in a few moments. These two assets of journaling and meditation go hand in hand. You will find that there are mediums or psychics out there who say you do not need a lot of what I am going to be teaching you. True, you do not need to on that level. But then again, are you ready to step up to the next level of your own evolution? I am going to assist and guide you to a higher level of your development, and, yes, it is needed. The Blessed Mother has shown me what the "Children of the New Jerusalem" will be needing along their way, and she has always guided me with love and truth. What she has given all of us with the simplicity of her words is so easy to do that you will be making it a part of your life and in no time you will be wondering how you ever lived without it.

How do you feel after doing this exercise? I know this is sometimes hard, and to many it will not be that bad. As I said before, I will be tweaking you along the way. This work will be integrated into your life in such a way that at first it might seem hard. However, once you lay your foundation down, you will only continue to grow.

You are going to find where journaling is a huge part of your life in who you are. It can be your best friend as you write out your thoughts, feelings, emotions, concerns, etc. To top it all off, you will be giving so much to the words you write that the words cannot come back to you.

I like to look at it like this: you go through your day – working, talking and doing. When you come home or have some down time to yourself, you then start to process all that has been given to you in your day, to assemble and dissect from everyone and everything you experienced in your day: conversations, business deals, traffic, family and friends, etc. Your exchange of thoughts is then processed in your mind over and over again as you try to remember each scenario. The thing is, these thoughts then start to be analyzed by your conscious mind and take on a life of their own. They start to work with your subconscious mind to figure them out. The next thing you know, you have what is called the "gossip effect," a mass discussion of thoughts that want to interpret and re-interpret your thoughts all on their own and go off in their own direction so that they are then unrecognizable from what was originally said. All of this is then stored in your brain and twisted in so many directions that your mind cannot calm down from what it is projecting to your conscious mind of thought. This also becomes a big contributor to stress, sleepless nights, addictions, etc., in the unsuccessful effort to stop this thought process which will then contribute to anxiety or depression. Example: You have a friend, and you tell them a secret. They then tell a friend, who then tells another and so on. By the time it comes back to you, it has gone in so many directions that you then feel sick because it is no longer the truth of what you originally said.

This is how we have been conditioned to think with our brain and how it works. What you will be doing is to take all of those thoughts out of your mind and place them on paper in a journal. How simple is that? Well, for some, real simple. However, for others, it will take some time, and that is okay as long as you are trying. With each step you take, it becomes easier and easier. It is all up to you and what you want in your life.

The next step is to ask: how do we write in our journals? Well, I have tried it so many ways that my guides came to me and finally said, "What are you doing?" I said, "Writing in my journal." They proceeded to laugh and say, "Did not get too far, did you?" I was confused because here I had pages of stuff, so I said, "What in the world do you mean? I have over four hundred pages; I think that is pretty good." Then I hear, "but are you writing from your heart or your head?" I had to stop and think about it, and sure enough I was writing from my head; I was trying to control the contents of the pages to fit what I thought I wanted to hear. I asked, "Okay, how do I write in my journal about all of the things that are going on inside of my head, my life and my heart?" "Simple," was their reply. "Start each journal entry to the one who loves you the most." I sat there and started thinking. Well, I know who I want that I believe loves me the most, but then I have my husband, my children, my parents, etc. I asked, "This is one who loves me unconditionally and will never yell or put me down, right?" Then I saw the most brilliant lights in front of me that just felt so warm and loving. I started writing, "Dear Heavenly Father Mother God, thank you for this day and all the gifts of this day. Today the clouds are so close and near; I can feel you here with me, and I thank you. Did you see what happened as I ………….." After about an hour, my guides came through and said:

> "Now, doesn't it feel good to write from the heart to the one who will never judge you and loves you so much? You see, God already knows your heart. What you do not want to give to others, God already has accepted you for the truths and sees your compassion to everyone in your heart. God knows what you are ashamed of and what matters to you the most. God knows every secret you have and has never told anyone. God loves you for who you are."

To this day, in my own journaling and what I always teach others to write is what was exactly given to me. You see, you are starting your true relationship and having a conversation with God, one who loves you unconditionally, never judges you and will never tell your secrets. God has already known everything there is about you and what you have been through for a very long time. This will be an intimate time for you, getting to know the one you have always had questions about. Your questions will be answered as you release that which you hold in your mind. In my journaling, I talk about everything even if I think it is stupid, crazy, foolish, embarrassing and so on, for I know that I have the greatest of friends in God.

When you look at what you are writing, you next need to take some steps here also as in your day to day life, your relationships, your worries and problems. You are going to move toward releasing and forgiveness. What are you releasing? What are you forgiving? I am so glad you asked. You will be releasing years of issues, anger, sadness, fears and resentments. You will be taking a step back in time and looking at your life on all levels: things that have bothered you, made you angry, hurt you, made you smile, laugh and have brought joy into your life; the individuals that you have had relationships with who may still be in your life or may not be in your life. Then you are going to forgive them, honestly and truly from deep within your heart. The biggest thing you will be doing is – forgiving yourself! This is going to be asking you to have faith in all you do, faith in yourself and in God, faith in knowing everything that you will be doing. Everything that you will be going through and experiencing will be the true light of all that there is, knowing in that moment of time as you are forgiving the individual and yourself all of the pain, anguish, feelings, emotions. Any suffering will be taken from you as you place it in the hands of God. By releasing and giving all of it to your best friend GOD, you will be opening yourself up to the higher meaning of your life, the purpose of who you are here to be and what your true journey is all about. This is the first of the basic steps you will need to follow to make yourself a clear and clean vehicle. You will then need to have a foundation in your journaling to guide your development as you advance through this process.

This is how you look on a spiritual level as you start these steps of building your foundation: an onion. The proverbial onion, which has so many layers, is what I call society's conditioning and the "veils." You are the center seed. Each time you have gone through an episode in your life, you have added another veil or layer of the onion. As time goes by in your life, you are hugely covered from head to toe.

Now, with each issue and resentment you write about

honestly and really take the time to look at, you take the steps to forgive the other and forgive yourself. Then release it to God, and a layer or veil comes off. Your life is going to be unbalanced at first. Remember, with each layer, your body is starting to re-acclimate itself to its true state of being as when you were in spirit form before coming here to Mother Earth. The friends in your life will no longer be there or change; this can be good or hard, and will be a test to see if you are really ready to do the work. Just remember, everything that you get rid of in your life that is not in integrity, you will then gain that much and more than you can imagine. As you keep clearing these veils or layers from you, you start to shine in your own ascension of self. You will feel lighter, love more and appreciate that which is within you and around you. You will then open the doors to the heavens above.

I have numerous students and clients who later in the years of their own development have come up to me and said, "Adele, I thought I was doing the work with my journaling, but the biggest thing I did not really do was take the time to really look at what the journaling really meant to me as a person." I let the individual tell their story from their perspective to help assist them further to acknowledge that, yes, they are truly ready to begin now and get through that which they need to.

Now all of this takes us back to what I call the "Band-Aid effect." So many individuals have placed Band-Aids on their issues, problems or life stories, and they are really afraid to lift this band aid off everything. You know how it feels as you try to lift the band aid off an injured area. You start to peel it back and "ouch," that hurts a little. You either leave it alone, start pulling it as gently as possible, or, for the brave soul out there, you rip it off in one shot. Which one are you? Will you just leave it alone and go on? Will you gently pull the band aid little by little? Or will you rip it off in one huge motion?

The choice is up to you. I want you to remember in all of this that you have asked to understand your own journey in this life. You have asked to understand your spiritual awakening and what it all entails, and you have asked "How do I develop my gifts and abilities so that we may then guide, assist and help one another in this lifetime?"

Let's start with some basic steps. Make a list of each and every resentment which is an issue that you hold within your mind to forgive each and every thing. Clear the fragments of that which you are holding onto that you have focused on for so long, to bring consciously up close to your awareness that which is what is holding onto you that you have not yet forgiven. This will include the most important family members, friends, partners, acquaintances, work associates, teachers, and events in your life. Keep each one of these listed on a separate page of your journal as you will go back to each one.

You will need to begin writing about your childhood because this is the most significant area of your life that brings forth the deepest of issues, the most emotional baggage that you have carried around for so long and that has contributed to who you are in its conditioning of family, friends and society.

Now, I know most if you will say: "I have already done this" or "I had a great childhood." To you I say, "Wonderful! Now go back and re-look at all areas again. If there is nothing that comes up and you have no issues, congratulations. You have done exceptionally well and should by now be well on your journey to success." I will also tell you to take just one more look. If you have done all this and have not written in your journal for awhile, then you, my friend, have issues that you have then created to be in your past once again. You see, you have this book in your hands for a reason, and your guides, angels, teachers and loved ones want you to have it for that very reason!

Okay, now take one issue/resentment at a time and start writing everything down you associate and remember with it. Take a deep look inside yourself as you do so, and remember there are two sides to every story. You must be totally honest with yourself in this area, and you will be looking at each issue and resentment to see how you also contributed to the situation surrounding its creation. Close your eyes and see, feel and know what went on during that time; see yourself as you step back in time and acknowledge the truth. As you do so, you will start to see the other person, place, situation or thing in its own truth. When looking at it from all of these sides, you will start to see how it all truthfully played out, even the truth of your own involvement. As I said, there are two sides of every story, and yes, this means you had a side/hand in the situation also, no matter what it may be. Write down all that you feel, see, sense, hear and know. It is all being given to you, so just relax and let go; let yourself become one with that situation again. From this moment on, you will begin to break down and examine your resentments and issues.

I acknowledge that this can be very hard to do. It is a very emotional time as you will be bringing things up that you have long ago hidden deep inside. Remember at the very core of who you are, is the heart of fear; fear is all that is standing in the way. You have held onto this fear for so long it has now become one with you and will do whatever it can to stay near and dear. This fear also has at its core major issues of your life in these areas: your relationships with your spouse, partner, mother, father, children, friends; your ego or self-esteem; your sense of security, peace and balance. You need to realize and understand this to acknowledge all that there is before you, as you begin moving forward.

This will be a time of mourning. To respect this grief process that you will be going through is to honor yourself along the way. A time when that belief, hurt, pain, and the association to the issue and resentment that you have held onto for so long will finally die, and you can and will be able to start to breathe and live easier in your life.

I will say this to you now. If you are going through all of this and there is no emotion, no emotional release, then you are not touching that part of your heart and soul to release it. You are not being totally honest with yourself and that to which you hold dear. There is no better time than now to take these steps to your own ascension. Just ask God to be there listening as you do; remember, God has already heard it and seen it with you for all of this time. What are a few more moments to seeing it through and releasing it forever?

As you are going back in time to your childhood and through this mourning process, you will be seeing the difference in this issue being played out in a whole new light of understanding. There will be major players in this area that you are dealing with, and there will be revelations to the ones that you did not consider being a part of it. Your guides will be there helping you to understand why you keep thinking of someone from that same time period of the issue even though you do not remember them being part of the issue. For now, you will be seeing the reality of the whole thing. Maybe there was another person that you had no interaction with, but they were a part of the issue nonetheless. In this new light, you can start to piece together what really did happen at that time in your life in a way that speaks of the truth as you really know it on a soul level and one with God. Keep writing until you have all of the associated pains, hurts, fears, and emotions drained from you, and then take a moment to BREATHE.

Just sit back, relax and breathe.

Now, I want you to take a good look at how this particular issue and resentment played a role in your life up until this moment. Write about how it prohibited your life in such a way as you gave more power and strength to it to control you in any way and kept you from truly enjoying your life. How the peace that is inside of you was given way to another.

The final step in this process as you have successfully broken down the issue and resentment is for you to truly forgive. Forgive the other person in all of this truthfully from the depth of your soul, as you will be experiencing a whole new understanding to this person and who they actually are and how they themselves had their own resentments and issues in their own lives but did not have the chance at that point to have something or someone to assist them in releasing the fear from inside their own self. Then truly forgive yourself. As you forgive yourself, give everything over to God. Ask God to take all of it. As you do, you will feel a lifting deep inside of you that just washes over your whole body; you will know that you are cleansed of this issue and resentment forever in the heart of God. God has been waiting for you to do just that, to trust enough to accept yourself as God accepts you, to Love yourself as God loves you and to be one with God in all things.

As you step back in this process and take a look at the larger picture, have fun and write about the positive outcomes this issue and resentment brought to you in your life right now and the complete positive that will now be a part of your life from experiencing and doing all of this. You may now look at this in a whole new way of living, for this is living spiritually. A calmness of love and happiness washes over you, and you feel it inside for the first time in a long time. You have been working on your own transformation, and the happiness it brings has no words.

Chapter XI

The Miracles of Meditation

I would now like to guide everyone in taking the time to see and understand what mediation and development are. I receive so many calls and mail from individuals who want to learn how to meditate and develop themselves, but they do not have any place to go or understand all that is involved or have no teacher around them. In times like these, "When the student is ready, the teacher shall appear." I am going to take you a little more into what is involved in meditation and spiritual mediumship development. This will not be a total substitute for my classes and workshops. However, with this book you have in your hands right now, I give you the basic foundation for all you need in your own spiritual and mediumship development, to help you gain an understanding of what to do and what is expected as you prepare yourself for your "teacher."

The development classes and workshops that I teach are a combination of Old School and New School, with a spiritual approach guided by the Blessed Mother. She is preparing the way for the teachers, so the "New Jerusalem" will be at hand for the calling of the veils when we will all be approached and absorbed by the light of God. My work is to teach Teachers of this Light.

We are as fortunate in these times as any because this has been for quite awhile the ushering in, as you all know, of the divine feminine energies. This, in time, started with the revival of "Diana," and what could be a greater feminine representation of that energy than Princess Diana? As we all fell in love with this young lady, we added her into our lives with opened hearts. She in her own symbology stood for so many of us in all sectors of our lives, and we related to her on so many levels. She in her innocence brought to us the doors that opened the divine feminine energies, and they have kept opening up the greatest flood of energies as we transitioned and shape-shifted from one of masculine energy to a balance that which will make it complete.

So welcome, as we have marked the times to be of our greatest learning and advancement of ascension of our times. With this new school of development that we are doing and bringing "across the miles" with the hierarchy of divine guidance, there is The Blessed Mother the Divine Feminine.

I teach my students with these words: "She is here with us. She is guiding and answering the call of placement of those who have been longing and waiting for these times." This is also in part why so many individuals are feeling a calling for higher learning to be a part of something that has been forbidden or just out of their reach. Well, no more, as you have everything in front of you that there is to hear that calling and move forward. It is up to you to step out and do!

There may not be a teacher right now near you. There may not be that place to go and develop, but there is that which is in you that will know what to do. I have been guided and working on that which is needed in the easiest format for you to learn. You must remember there are no short cuts; there is a foundation which must be learned. If there is no foundation, then the learning you do is going to stay at the level in which you learned it. Faith, Prayer, Love, Focus, Integrity, Responsibility and Honesty shall always be in place for your steps to take you in the right direction.

Most of us have had at some point in our lives some strange things happen. It makes us more aware of what we perceive as normal and what is not. Now, some dismiss the things that are going on; others decide they want to learn and understand more.

Development is taking the time to just sit and get to know who you are as a physical person and who you are as spirit form. Your goal is to begin training through awareness, focus and disciplining the various levels of yourself: the physical, the emotional, and the everyday personality. Learning to focus and bring these three levels together is the challenge in all of it. As we are meditating, we are not just making our minds empty. We are intentionally bringing our level of awareness up through the raising of our vibrations. Everything resonates at a level of awareness of vibration, even spirit, which vibrates more at a higher level of frequency than we are. Then, it is taking the time utilizing meditation to raise our vibration to come to a compromise of fine-tuning of vibrations to recognize one another. As we do, we are opening ourselves up to the spirit self and those in spirit to allow ourselves to be comfortable to make that connection.

We have a host of guides, teachers and loved ones in spirit who are working with us at all times to assist and guide us all the way. You have been introduced to them in the preceding chapters. It is up to the individual to allow and give their self permission to relax and be one at the higher vibration for spirit communication. Meditation is the most important aspect of this work and not to be taken lightly. You may meditate with soft music, quietness, chanting or a ringing of a bell to start you. It is what makes you comfortable and relaxed. Sometimes I play music very softly where I barely hear it. Sometimes I turn the volume up so high that it vibrates through my house. Sometimes I sit among the tress and flowers and smell the sweet scent and softness of Mother Earth, the bounty of nature all around me, as I let myself go. It is all a personal thing and what you want to do in the meditation.

During this time of initial connection, there are other basic foundations that must be established, "Rules of Law," you might say, to further you along.

"For in each individual who recognizes the need to open themselves and develop that which they seek, there are responsibilities that go hand in hand together!" Adele

When we meditate, we are also working with the breath. This is very important as you will be learning how to breathe to where you will feel as if you are not breathing at all. As you go into meditation, be aware of your breathing. With each inhale and each exhale, as you focus your mind on your breathing, you will be giving yourself permission to relax and to let go. Keeping your awareness on the breath as it enters your body, feel the vibration of the breath as it fills you up and moves through your whole body. Continue in this breathing for five minutes. It is relaxing and letting your body know it is okay to relax and let go, an acclimation from the world of the physical to that of the spirit self. It is allowing yourself to let go of all things physical, including your physical body, physical thought patterns. Let go and just be.

As you go into your meditation, relaxing and breathing, do not try to empty your whole mind. Instead, as things come up, acknowledge it briefly, then see it enveloped in a beautiful green ball of light and let it go up into the universe. Keep aware of each inhale and exhale; give your shoulders permission to relax. Then start at your toes and let them relax. Go to your calves and knees, letting them relax. See the muscles let loose and be relaxed as you continue up your entire body, recognizing each area and then letting go of it, relaxing. Set your intentions for the meditation. At this point, when you first start to meditate, your intention will be to just relax and learn how to take these everyday thoughts, place then in the green light and let them float to the universe. After a period of practicing this, in your next meditation your intention should be on your breathing, one to help you raise your vibrations and then to learn your body. Learn how your toes feel, your legs, stomach, waist and so on until you have gotten to know your real body and self. This is not done in one meditation but may take several. Be patient with yourself. You are learning how to focus and undo years of thought forms as to what to be, just know you are being that which you truly are. As with each meditation, your body will start to recognize what you are asking it to do; and the flow will begin. Get to know your body. These first meditations should take you about fifteen to twenty minutes. Try not to push yourself, for you are learning so much during these times. As in all meditations, there is no right way of doing it. What you are experiencing is what you are experiencing, and everyone will be different in that regard.

Now, have a journal handy and write; write about your experience after your meditation. It is okay to say, "I am not sure I am doing any of this right, but I am doing it!" Write about what area or part of the meditation that you feel you did a great job with, how you felt about doing it and how much you are learning of yourself and your body. Once you have learned and mastered your own body and knowing your own vibration of energy, you will then move on to meet your guides, angels, teachers and loved ones in spirit.

I believe one of the biggest differences my students see with me as a teacher is that I am very clear about what they need to do to be a medium, psychic, teacher, spiritual being or whatever their heart is calling them to do. This is not to be taken lightly. You have a responsibility to so many. There are steps to take. You need an absolute foundation, and from there you build upon it in your own ascension. I take who I am very sincerely, for this is who I am no matter what time of day or night it is or what I am doing.

As a student in college, you go to class and apply yourselves in study. As you do so, you receive a grade and graduate with honors and degrees. You are applying and working toward a goal of who you are to be. That is the same thing I do; I apply that which I am and the work that I do with spirit as they guide and teach me to be who I am here to be. If that means mediating hours a day, then it is a delight to do so. With all of this, it is just what comes as naturally as each breath I breathe – praying, meditating, thanking God for the day, a moment in the day, blessing those I meet or have not yet met, being there with an open mind and heart, sharing, sending love and receiving love, etc.

As we apply all we learn in development, we are allowing ourselves to be of greater service in the light, to be a servant in God's name. This work is a selfless one that is in each and every one of us. Can you hear your heart calling? Can you hear spirit calling to you? Take twenty to thirty minutes a day to set aside to meditate. Become one within yourself and leave the rest to God, for he shall send his Angelic Ones to you to transport you to where you need to be. Be ready to open the door of opportunity when it comes. You will never forget it.

"A Spiritual Development Journey is one that you take to know thyself, of getting to experience and know who you really are in spirit form." Blessings, Adele

Chapter XII

The Spiritual Realms Of Your Guides and Teachers

This is a personal favorite chapter of mine. As I sit here and write, I get to introduce you to the specific guides, angels and teachers you have in spirit who work with you on different levels of your learning and work. Each guide who is with you deserves your honesty, trust, friendship and laughter along the way. As you meet them, get to know them and learn how you may work together in all areas of your life. As I said before, my guides are my best friends. As you develop your relationships with yours, I pray that you will allow them to be your best friends also.

I can't say often enough how important it is to understand what is going on around you as you work with spirit. Who is with you? What do they look like? What do they do with us? Why are they in our lives? How can you tell when they are around? As I considered questions like these, I needed to sit down with my counsel of Angelic Wise Ones and ask. This is by no means all of what they had to say. We will save part of that for another time. I am giving you what I hope is the best information I can give at this time on just a handful of the most well known spirit guides, angels and teachers that you will hear and work with the most. As in all things, please take what resonates with you. I am only an authority of what I know, how my relationships are with them and from my experiences throughout my life. You will meet many others in similar fields of work who might agree or disagree; my job is to teach you as much as I can on what I know and have always experienced.

Even though some would call me a psychic or medium, I really do not fit into that category. That is why my counsel of guides chose to call me a *Visionary Messenger*, in the truest sense, as I can see so much with anything you place in front of me. Yes, I can see, hear, sense, feel, smell and know each in spirit around me as a medium does, but I have expanded capabilities that I find most do not. And it is just that which I am bringing to you to discover within yourself. I want to help you to understand that this took me years of self-discovery, being around a variety of individuals with gifts and abilities, before I could see that I am unique. In saying this, I want you to understand that you are also unique. Just because you find yourself experiencing things that are different from what is the so-called norm of this profession does not mean anyone is any better than you or you do not have anything to offer. This place we live in can be very unforgiving to each of us. It is what you make of it and what you do with the knowledge and information about your own abilities. Also, after years of trying to fit in or just being surrounded by wonderfully gifted individuals in their own right, I can tell you that you need to understand this is a spiritual journey of the soul, a time of enlightenment of who you are. As you walk your journey, there will be those who, for one reason or another, will be jealous of you and try their best to keep you far under who they believe you to be so that you then start to adopt those same ideas and keep yourself down. This time in our history is not the time for you to stay down; it is the time for you to rise above that which society has told you. You need to be and live who you know you are deep down inside. This I know you understand.

As you sit here and read this book, you have that person inside of you who is a great soul saying, "Why cannot they see me for me? This is who I am and want to be." So what is stopping you? Is society so great in their own thinking and beliefs that they are any different than you? I do not believe this; unfortunately, at one time I did. Everyone is ready in their own time, but The Blessed Mother said to me many years ago, *"The time is coming when the children will start to rise above that which they think is holding them back, and as they do, they will walk to the light and ask why they did not do this before."* As the time came closer, she said I would have those who she will send to me to learn and prepare the way for a multitude of others to follow. She did; I have the finest students who I am working with and who are professionals in their own right. They have absorbed so much these past years and are brilliant in who they are and what they do. As I write these pages, she is here with me guiding me along my way. We are at the time in which we are opening up at a greater speed. The learning is before us like never before, and we have a choice in this evolutionary time to just be as we see others be or do as we know what we are here to do. I am choosing to "do" and follow the guidance before me, as I welcome you who have chosen to do the same in learning from the pages of this book.

Remember the words of Jesus: *"For these things I do, you shall do greater than I."* In all of this I have said, when you get to the part of your life where you have chosen to be a part of a private reading with your chosen medium, not all guides and teachers will show up for that medium and the same guides and teachers will not always show up for different mediums. Mediums cannot and should never say they can just call a selected person in spirit with whom you wish to connect. Once you read more about your gatekeeper, you will understand.

In your lifetime, you will have many guides and teachers in spirit who will be working with you at one time or another. Your guardian angel and gatekeeper are the only ones with you from birth until you make your transition home. All of your other spirit guides and teachers come and work with you as you are experiencing different levels of knowledge and experiences of education. There are wide ranges of experiences that you have chosen to go through in this physical incarnation on Mother Earth.

Spirit guides influence many areas of our lives, personally, emotionally, professionally and spiritually. Whatever power and experience the spirit is familiar with or comfortable with from one of their own incarnations on earth will be the area of expertise in which their power will be felt the most when they work with us. I want you to realize that your guides and teachers in spirit are highly evolved beings with a vast arena of knowledge and proficiency. No matter what area of understanding they bring to you, from your joy guide to that of your master teacher, please give them the respect and compassion that they deserve. They have chosen to assist and guide you through this lifetime, and in doing so they will bring to the table a wealth of wisdom and awareness for everything you will need. As you open the door to them, your life will change, and it will change for the better as you let it. Yes, in this spiritual journey, you will learn and grow. You will have sorrow and pain. As you open yourself fully, you will have a wealth of love, compassion, direction, understanding, new opportunities and a host of more being given to you.

This I want you to know, as the same is true with spirits in general as in our loved ones who have transitioned home because they all hold on to their personal uniqueness when they make their transition into spirit. If they were shy, loving, rude, a smoker, talented, outspoken, peaceful, loud, giving or analytical , they are that same way in spirit. This is not to say that they have not changed, as they all do. It is just that this is how we remember our loved ones when they were here on earth with us, so this then is a recognizable personal individuality of themselves with which we can associate. When they want to give us a message or let us know when they are around, perhaps when we decide to visit a medium for a reading, that personality trait that we associate with our loved one is what they call upon. From time to time, I have loved ones in spirit who want to visit and are here for my clients and students. These are ones whom I have gotten to know, and they will then be presenting themselves to me in a familiar way but also in a way that shows their own growth in their own realms of experience. I will give the message they are giving me. If the client will not accept it because it is not the way their loved one acted in this life, I have to go back and ask them to show me their former self here on earth. Sometimes the loved one will refuse or be annoyed as their loved one needs to understand they have also grown in this time period. Most of the time, they will smile or laugh at the infancy of development their loved ones here have and show me what they need to show to be recognized. This makes for a very funny and sticky situation, being stuck in the middle of a family dispute.

Spirit guides and teachers with similar characteristics to us are drawn to us; frequently they will share the same interest, have similar personality traits and may have worked in the same profession as we are in right now. This is also true for ones in spirit who are not our guides or teachers but who see the similarity of light we share with them and so stop by and visit with us. Once, I had a missionary who appeared beside me and presented himself on a spirit silk I have. It was awesome because at that moment in time I was working on a mission with abused women and children. The similarities of what we both love to do became apparent to this individual in spirit (by recognizing and being drawn to my light), and he just wanted to stop in and say hello, to see what I was working on. Somewhere within this coming together, there are going to be similarities that you will find between you and those in spirit.

You will find doctor guides assisting those who work in the healing professions, including spiritual healers, doctors, scientists and especially nurses. We attract to us that which is similar. Some believe they need only seek the ascended masters in searching for guidance in all they do, and there is nothing wrong with that. I also know that we have made contracts with many guides and teachers from the spiritual realms for our incarnation this lifetime to work with us in our spiritual journey, and it would be a shame not to also acknowledge and seek their counsel. They have their specific work to do with us in our learning/educational path. These are the ones I call my Counsel, and you will find that which best describes yours.

Following are descriptions and guidance related to working with our guides, teachers and angels. It is meant to be an enlightening means to work from and not intended to be limited in any way with those around us. It is just that we have so many individual guides around us. This is a great place to start, with the ones who are with us the most. The titles given to these guides, angels and teachers are for identification reasons only. By no means is it in any way descriptions of all of the guides, teachers and angels in spirit who work with us and lend a helping hand. When you visit or accept a message from a medium or directly from spirit, these are the most common names that will be connected to them and will be described to you in the delivery of your message. Please use the following as a guideline in the area of guidance you receive as you decide to work with or understand your messages, signs, symbols and gifts from one or more in spirit.

Please take what resonates with you in all things!!! As in all things, the more we work to get to know our guides and teachers, the more we will recognize their energy. We have some guides and teachers who will be with us for a long period of time and some who will not. Remember, the guides and teachers who are with you now in this moment are the ones who are with you as you go through a learning and developing phase of your life. When that growth of learning and development is through, you will both have a time period together as they help with the acquisition of your new guide and/or teacher in their place. When you feel that someone new is hanging out around you but cannot clearly make them out, this just may be a new guide or teacher waiting to come in. I have many guides who have been with me for so long, but I also have those who have worked with me as I feel a new energy around and slowly help me to get to know them. Then one day, when I ask my guide a question, they will bow to me, step back, turn around and walk away. As this happens, my new guide or teacher will present themselves with a large hug and smile, and I welcome them. At times like this, it is very warming and heartbreaking at the same time. I cannot anguish in this as this day has come, and I have marked a new milestone of ascension in my work and learning. I honor my departing guide and thank them for all of their love, guidance and support. I know if and when I really needed them, they would come forward to assist me; then again, I would only be asking them to walk away from their own growth and then start to hold myself back.

It is not the most important thing to have names from your guides, teachers and angels as long as you recognize them, work with them and ask for their assistance and guidance in all that you need. They are just waiting to have you acknowledge them, and they lovingly send their support willingly.

I think the biggest part after getting to know your guides, angels and teachers is the process of understanding the work you will be doing together from then on. As you establish this relationship, you will need to understand that they too are ascending, growing and learning in their realm of existence. My guides want to make sure you understand this, for you each have chosen one another to assist, guide, teach, support, nurture, protect and love in your individualized evolution in your own realms of existence. This is how it works; this is why they are called guides and teachers. They have so much work to do in their own realms and have a level of learning they are trying to do at the same time as working with you, so both of you are working towards the same goals – ascension to the next level of existence.

Now, I also want to mention spirit students of your guides and teachers. These are individuals in spirit who are at your physical level of growth and development. They are ones who are learning side by side with you with the same guide and teacher as you but in spirit. If you have been told you have two teacher guides and only know of one, or one steps back from you but does not necessarily have anything to give you, then he most likely is a student guide, learning from your teacher guide to be a teacher guide in spirit to another one here on earth. Guides have no gender as we would believe them to have. Remember, just as we have both male and feminine energy so too do your guides, angels and teachers. If you and a friend are working together in getting to know your counsel and you have a male protector guide and they have a female protector guide, that is great and as it should be. It is the guide's dominant energy coming across for you to know and understand. I have a friend who has a female protector guide with her, and she looks like Zena, a female warrior from the 1700s. As she works with my friend, she is also supporting her in her choices of who she is.

As I said earlier, they will have similarities with you, which makes it easier for you to get to know them and educate you in yourself. If you have your heart set on a female and a male shows up as a guide, relax and enjoy what you will be taught as you get to know one another. The first guides and teachers one usually meets is the *protector guide* and *joy guide*. This is one way of saying we need joy in our life as we look for protection in all we do. Then the *gatekeeper* comes in with your *guardian angel*. The *doctor teacher guide* is next, and the rest follow soon after as they watch how receptive you are working with everyone else. This is not to say that this is written in stone this way. Some may meet their gatekeeper and guardian angel first; it is all up to the individual and their learning.

The Joy Guide

The Joy Guide most often appears as a child, a small fairy-like child and/or young maidenly adolescent. They can display behavior that would be described as mischievous. Your Joy Guide is the one who is responsible for bringing out the lighter side of your personality. When things become missing, your Joy Guide is there to let you know to lighten it up. Even though your Joy Guide appears to be childish in many ways, be respectful to them, for your Joy Guide is highly intelligent in all ways, which is true of all your guides. When mirth and merriment manifest within a group of people unexpectedly for no particular reason, it is frequently the presence of someone's Joy Guide causing the frivolity and trying to get your attention. We could all certainly benefit from less stress by viewing some matters with a sense of humor.

Call upon your Joy Guide when your daily life becomes overwhelming, and you need to laugh out loud. Your Joy Guide will show you the humor in the situation. This Joy Guide is sometimes referred to as a medium's "message bearer" and to help control the spirit crowd of an individual who is seeking a reading or channeling. Your Joy Guide may sometimes call you "Mommy" as she is of that childlike energy and wanting to make you happy and joyful.

I work with my Joy Guide in delivering all my messages as she controls the crowd in spirit and lets them know what my "rules" are when I work. In my workshops and classes, she gathers other Joy Guides together to keep them busy and gives them the outline of what we will be doing. Together then, they all come together to bring a lightness of energy when we need it. She is also my "hostess with the mostess" as she welcomes all who enter our home and greets everyone's guides, angels, teachers and loved ones in spirit from the light, letting them know what is going on and who needs to do what.

The Protector Guide

The Protector Guide, seems to be the guide everyone is most familiar with and expects to work with and hear from when in a private session with a medium. Since the Native American Indian is the true native of the United States, it is the Native American Indian who appears most often. As I have said, I have a friend who has a female protector guide with her who looks like Zena, a female warrior from the 1700s. More likely than not, you will have a Native American Indian. If you are from Africa, you might have one who looks like an African Warrior; from Sweden, you might have one who looks like a Viking. Be relaxed and receive your guide in whatever form they show you.

Your Protector Guide is usually the first one to make a strong presence with you because you are more comfortable with their protective nature spirit. I have found that most Protector Guides work with those who are balanced and connect with Mother Earth in one way or another, from everyday yard work to planting and working with herbs. So go ahead and work with the soil of Mother Earth. Go to an area that has a small pond, stream or lake and get to know the area; take notice of the plants in your yard and neighborhood. As you do so, you will notice your Protector Guide presence around you. As you are examine the local plants, you will begin to understand all about them and find yourself thirsting to know more. This is the influence of your Protector Guide.

Many people feel the presence of their Protector Guide sitting next to them in a car when they travel, and some tell stories about accidents being averted due to their Indian guides. My Protector Guide is my first and most trusted best friend, who never leaves my side and always looks out for my best interest in my work. When I lay down to go to sleep at night, I ask him to be at my side and watch over me as I sleep and dream, that no harm may come to me.

The Gatekeeper

The first guide in the band is called Gatekeeper or Doorkeeper. The Gatekeeper is one of only two of your guides who are with you from birth to transition.

The Gatekeeper guide is one of my much-loved guides (as they all are), Your Gatekeeper is the guide who gives his consent or non-consent to the visiting clients – guides, teachers and loved ones in spirit – to communicate in a reading with the medium, or yourself as the practicing medium.

Your Gatekeeper is with you from birth until you make your transition home just as your Guardian Angel is. Please do not confuse the two of them, for they are totally different. This spirit guide is your overall protector in your life work and in what you are here to do. The Gatekeeper looks over and watches out for your best interest and holds you close so no harm may come to you. Very often when you see a Gatekeeper Guide around someone, the guide will stand behind or in front of that person wearing a voluminous cape with lots of enveloping folds. This guide will wrap the cape around the individual, which automatically signals a feeling of protection and identifies the guide as a gatekeeper. You also will find that the Gatekeeper will have characteristics similar to your own or a feeling of familiarity as with a past life. Your Gatekeeper knows every life lesson you are here to learn and has contracted with you to make sure you earn those lessons. Even with free will of choice, your Gatekeeper is here to make sure everything goes accordingly to your contract.

Please note that if you have a client in front of you who wants you to connect with their mom in spirit, and your Gatekeeper says no, then you cannot call their mom on the spirit phone and say, "Hello, Mom." The Gatekeeper's main job is to make sure you and/or your client is receiving the message they are there to receive. If anyone tells you different, that they can connect up and get your mom, to me, this is misleading. You have been guided to connect to a medium, psychic, etc., to receive a delivery of a message that you need to know. It is up to the Gatekeeper to make sure the message is delivered to you in what you need to know. If and when the message is delivered and you understand, then the Gatekeeper gives entry to your loved one or mom. Now, this is not to say that your mom might be the very one who is to deliver your message, and then you will be able to have that connection. Remember, it is what you are there to know and hear, not always what you want to hear and know. I go back again and say that if you call to make an appointment for a reading or deliverance of messages and someone says that, yes, they can connect you to your mom, I do not know anyone that can guarantee to do this. Please look for another avenue to receive your reading.

The Doctor Teacher Guide

The Doctor Teacher Guide, also referred to as the physician, M.D., medical or psychologist, plays the most prominent role with those who work in a healing profession, such as doctors, nurses, veterinarians, ministers or spiritual healers. This guide, however, also will assist those who work in other realms., as in a Philosopher Doctor Teacher guide. You may at any one time have anywhere from one to four doctor guides, or more, depending on what is going on in your life. Many physical mediums have their Doctor Teacher Guide as their main guide in their work. Also, Doctor Teacher Guides are not limited to those in the medical profession, as many Doctor Teacher Guides do not have a medical degree from their many incarnated lifetimes but have the doctor degree for the amount of work that they have achieved in all of their lifetimes to honor them with the title of doctor.

Everyone I have met does have a medical doctor guide, one who works with them when guiding assistance is needed when health questions come up or when seeking out a physical doctor who will help them with their own special needed assistance of medical care. Each of us has the ability to "feel" an area of our body that needs attention. Through meditation, we can communicate with our Doctor Teacher Guide in order to receive information regarding what may be wrong with our body, what course of action to take when we develop a condition and which physical doctor we need to see for the condition. The information you receive can vary from starting to exercise to changing your diet, checking your medications, seeking spiritual counseling or visiting a physical medical doctor. My Doctor Teacher Guides assist me with my healthcare all the way up to the visionary messages I receive and relay to the recipient.

The Chemist Teacher Guide

Physical Phenomena was quite popular from the 1850s through the 1920s as a means to prove the continuity of life and the ability to communicate with the spirit world. It was the Chemist Teacher Guide who adjusted the medium's body to accommodate the physically exhausting channeling of spirit entities that were necessary to perform such phenomena as materialization of spirits and floating trumpets. Ectoplasm is necessary to produce the phenomena, and the Chemist is the spirit who made the adjustment within the medium to produce it.

Our body chemistry has changed so much due to the medicines prescribed for us that I hear a lot of talk about how our bodies are not conducive as they once were for the channeling of spirit phenomena. The chemically preserved foods we eat and the quality of our environment, as well as our own conditioning from outside influences, have affected our abilities. Does this mean that no one has a Chemist Teacher Guide in his or her band? No! We all have Chemist Teacher Guides; they just work with us in other ways as we look at our medicines, food and all health-related issues in how we choose to live. The more you make yourself aware of what is going on in your body and make the choice to live in a clean and clear body, the more active your Chemist Teacher Guide becomes as he sees the work you are doing to preserve yourself in wanting to work with him. Anyone at any time can start to develop their relationship with their Chemist Teacher Guide by changing the way they live and eat and then meditating to open up the channel of communication. I sometimes recommend to a handful of my students who want to discipline themselves so they can work with their Chemist doctors to sit for at least two-to-four hours a day.

The Master Teacher

This is a very special guide to me for all the work I have always done. The Master Teacher imparts to us spiritual wisdom and philosophy, and it frequently has a Far East appearance. Your Master Teacher may appear as Asian, Hindu, a Buddhist monk or someone representative of India. I have even had a Moroccan Master Teacher. For a person studying a spiritual path, this guide is of great importance. For some, this guide may be overlooked, while others become fixated with their Master Teacher, seeing it as their one and only guide. Some even suggest that if you do not know your Master Teacher, you don't know your guides. Well, I am here to say that simply is not true. We work with and know our guides when we need to, and as we work more and more with them, we get to know them better. As you work in some capacity within the spiritual or metaphysical world, the guidance you receive from your Master Teacher will help you to acquire more of a spiritual awareness and a discernment of life in general. People who are associated with a mission for humanity and animals or other humane causes certainly are strongly influenced by their Master Teachers in all they do. The Master Teacher seems to come in around highly religious people, or the missionary who fights for a worthy cause, one who is never alone in all of the work they are here to do.

Ascended Masters

Ascended Masters are highly evolved beings who have fulfilled their karma through many incarnations on the earth plane and have continued to evolve on the spirit side/spiritual realms to become the enlightened beings that they are. Most see these Ascended Masters as high vibratory energies of light, and others see them as they would appear in the physical form from their many incarnations. They lovingly assist all of us spiritually, whether we are a spirit embodied within the human form or a spirit who has made the transition to the other side of life. All of us may call upon any of the universal Ascended Masters when we feel the need for their services. As with all our guides and teachers, each Ascended Master has their area of expertise in which they work with us. Some examples of Ascended Masters would be The Blessed Mother, Lord Kuthumi, Saint Germaine, Jesus, Lady Kwan Yin, Saint Joseph, Master Buddha and Saint John Of God. As in all things, one can cultivate a relationship with the Universal Ascended Masters through prayer, meditation and petitions of assistance. When the Ascended Masters are present, you will feel their love, strength, peace and comforting presence all around you.

Guardian Angels

Is a Guardian Angel the same as a Spirit Guide or Teacher Guide? Well, Guardian Angels and angels are spiritual beings who are very present in our lives and in a class all by themselves. What makes them angelic is that they have never incarnated on Mother Earth, unlike our spirit guides and teachers.

Our personal Guardian Angel is with us from birth until we make our transition home, as is our Gatekeeper, although they are not to be confused with each other. Our Guardian Angel has never had a physical incarnation while our Gatekeeper Guides and teachers have had many a lifetime in physical form.

Our Guardian Angels are with us to keep us on our path of light so that when we may, by "free will of choice," wander away from our true divine path, the Guardian Angel will guide us back to where we need to be. When you are in a harmful situation that can cause you to transition before your time, it will be your Guardian Angel who yells out very audibly to you "No!" or "Do not go there, turn back!" This is such a strong, commanding voice that you will hear it, outside your body, next to you, so that it will make you jump or stop in your tracks. Listen to what your Guardian Angel says, and do it right away!

We are truly blessed to have so many in spirit to support us in our time here on Mother Earth, and I honor them all!!!

I hope you have gained some insight into the spiritual realms of all that is, all that was and all that ever will be, and that part of if not all of this information has helped you in your travels with spirit. As before, take what resonates with you. This list is by no means meant to be complete. When you need assistance and guidance in any form or fashion, your team of angels, guides, teachers and loved ones will be there for you. If there is anything that one of them cannot do, they will seek those who can be there for you.

Before I leave this subject, I want to mention our loved ones who have transitioned and then become a guide unto themselves to assist us. This seems to be a very controversial area that everyone likes to discuss but not give clear understanding on, so I am giving it my best shot. A loved one in spirit can be there to guide you; but if your mother transitioned, she is not automatically a guide like those I discussed earlier. Yes, she will help, assist and guide you on a much different level. As in all things, your loved one is there to let you know that they are okay, happy and fine. I call on my mother all the time with a situation with the family, and she comes right away and helps me. However, you must remember a few things.

Your loved ones in spirit are still learning and growing in spirit form and have much work themselves to do. Yes, they can be everywhere with everyone in the whole family at the same time, just as angels, guides and teachers can. In knowing your loved one so well, you will always have the physical attachments to them from the physical characteristics they themselves had when living here on earth, so you will always see them in that physical role without understanding that they are so much more now. They are learning at a level of their own ascension. I understand someone needing their loved one to be a guide to them after they transition, but they themselves are not always in the same category as your guides, angels and teachers. You would be amazed to know just what your loved ones are doing after they transition. Some are sitting on political boards of earthly concerns when it comes to all things that govern our political empires. I laugh and get such delight in thinking how it could be your aunt who only baked the best food in this life and wanted nothing to do with politics who suddenly has major influence in this arena. But who else would be better to have working for us? If she was the best cook, she will be the best at political affairs.

It is wonderful to have the best of memories of our loved ones. As we too go on with our lives, they too go on with theirs. They welcome it when we send out a calling to them to be at our sides. I remember one woman sitting with me who wanted to speak to her grandfather. He actually did come in and let her know he was busy just then, and he asked her flat-out what she was making such a ruckus about. Her life was good, and if she would get rid of the lazy husband she had it would be even better. This grandfather loved her, but he needed to keep his attention on other events going on. He was especially needed in the acclimation ward as one who just committed suicide was coming home. I am afraid to say the lady was so horrified that her grandfather was working with another individual. You see in this life, he did not like anyone very much. With all of that information, she ran out from our session without her purse so she could get home to tell her mother.

Then, there are those events when a famous person is transitioning home. My girlfriend told me of her friend in spirit who came through during a séance circle and informed her lovingly they were getting ready for someone very special to come home. She was very excited and could not possibly understand what he was talking about. The next day she heard Princess Diana had transitioned.

I love it when our loved ones get so involved in areas that we would not have expected from them as we look back and think about their own personalities here with us. It is more proof to me of the extended learning we do and are always doing. We just need to understand that, no, they are not just sitting beside us all of the time, though they are close to us whenever we need them.

Before you go on to read the next section, I invite you to take a moment to reflect on the importance of all your guides. Sit down and take a moment to gently quiet your mind with some deep, even breaths. Let go of the day. Say a small prayer to surround you in the light of the Holy Spirit and invite in all those loving guides, teachers and angels from the light to be with you. Ask them to share with you for your highest good, then just relax and watch what comes to you in the form of pictures, thoughts, impressions, smells, a knowing, sensing and feelings. When you are done with your relaxing time with all of them, please give thanks for their being with you and invite them to join you in all you do.

Welcome to the spiritual realm. May you be blessed forever!!!

Chapter XIII

Loved Ones in the Spirit Realms

I want to take some time to introduce to you what I have been given and shown about our loved ones in spirit. As you have read in the previous chapters, when I refer to the dying process, this is called transitioning, when our true soul or inner spirit leaves this physical body and purely goes home to that which was before this lifetime here on Mother Earth.

The transitioning process is not as complex as so many make it out to be. That is not to say that there isn't any other explanation but mine, but I just believe that it is quite an easy process no matter what way or means the process takes.

As our loved ones transition, they are enveloped by this beautiful golden white light. Around this beautiful golden white light is all of their loved ones, guides, angels, all those who they shared this experience of a physical life with who are already in the spiritual realms. There is no pain, no anguish of what the physical body is going through. Do you understand this? No matter what the experience of the physical death may be, our loved ones feel no pain! If it is in their contract to transition from whatever experience they are going through, then it is in their contract not to be associated with pain at that moment of time. God does not let his children suffer; it is the physical conditioning of society that makes us think this. I will say that when a loved one is in an accident and lives through it then, yes, they have pain; this pain lets them know they are still alive in the physical and have not crossed over. That is why you will see and hear individuals talk about their experience and the hurt and pain they felt so much. What they do not tell you is that at that moment of impact of what their physical bodies were going through to get them to that point, they did not feel a thing. Why? It was because their soul was re-looking at their contract. If it had said yes this is an "out," their own time to transition home, then they would transition. If it said no, they would be pulled back to the physicality of the world and feel all of the pain there is to feel from their physical body and what it had just gone through.

As the soul, the inner spirit transitions from the physical body. When our loved ones transition, they are immediately light in body and mind. They are at first surprised at the feeling and sensation as they are immediately in an area that is familiar, where they find themselves with the source of all things. To many, it may be with their loved ones. To others, it is with their Guardian Angel and Gatekeeper who are beside them as they are meeting that which they love the most. Many will experience different things and places. As we grow as an individual, we have many life teachings, which I call society's conditioning. If in those life teachings you believed a philosophy that said that when you transition you go to the pearly gates, then when you first transition you will go to the pearly gates.

In my own near-death experience, one minute I was at an intersection sitting in my car waiting for the green light when "BAM," a huge white light appeared before me; I was then sitting on the side of a mountain with Jesus. We were casually looking out over the city of Jerusalem, talking as if we had never left one another. When I consciously become aware of the differences around me, I laughed. The feeling I had at that moment was as if I had been there the whole time and had never left his side, and we were engaged in something that we would do on a daily basis, just as you visit a friend or family member for lunch or dinner. It was that easy, such a euphoric moment of time – surreal yet comfortably real. It is such a comfort and confirmation for me to know that when it is time to go home that it is as easy as just being in the reality we believe we are in right now.

This is the stage I call acclimation, where, right there and then, we immediately acknowledge our physical life and decide what needs to be done first for those who have always been called our family, those who we have just left behind in the physical world. Our loved ones who have transitioned then step back to help assist those who they know will need them the most and watch how things play out. This is usually a process that I have been shown over and over again to last about fourteen days. During that time, our loved ones to tie up lose ends and try to let their loved ones know they are okay and wipe away the tears they see them shed. If we have been left behind, they join us when there are the funeral arrangements to make, and they're with us at the funeral. Every time I go to a viewing or funeral, I see them standing by someone or talking about another individual that was a part of their physical life here. It's amazing to see them looking at the flowers that were sent, noting who made it to the funeral and who did not, hearing everyone talking about them, or crying or being strong in the face of personal loss. This is a joyous occasion to know that they are still so much a part of their loved ones' lives and that there is in no more pain for them. They are whole and happy. This time period is actually for those physically living to grieve and mourn, to go through the acclimation process in such a different way as their loved one was just taken from their life.

I want you to understand during this process of acclimation that their true soul, their inner spirit, is adjusting to being lighter and not having the cares, worries, depression, anger, sadness, etc., that they may have had before they transitioned. They are going through the process of seeing things in a much lighter viewpoint, with a tremendous amount of love for everyone. Are they still the same as when they were living with you? Yes, in personality, but they can see the bigger picture more than when they were living here with you. They can see what part of their own contract they had with you and everything that is before you yet to come for you to physically live through. It's as if you are at the scene of a volcano about to erupt, and you can see the whole thing happening and know what to expect before it actually does.

At the same time, they are adjusting in vibration back to that which they were before being born here on Mother Earth and getting acclimated to not having a dense physical body anymore to weigh them down. It is during this time that they are letting that inner child come out and rejoicing in the feelings.

As this happens, they are losing the density at a greater speed of light to then become whole and pure once again. The reviewing takes place. This is what most of you may be more familiar with regarding this process. The reviewing is the time to look at the contract that they had in place, the scripting of what their physical life was to be like here, their path in life. All of the learning that they needed to do as they were here, who they had arranged to be with in this lifetime for that learning, at what point their lives would intersect and what they were to accomplish in their learning with each and every different individual. And then what actually did take place in their physical lives: how far did they get with each learning assignment? What intersection did they veer off their path to see their life through their own loving eyes with no shading and nothing hidden from view? The reviewing also includes how they interacted with each individual they had in their physical lifetime, whether it was good or bad. Did they really enjoy who they were, all the way to seeing how their own actions were placed on someone else and how that affected that individual's life?

All of this is done in a very warm, loving gentle environment with their loved ones, guides, teachers and any religious figure whom they were devoted to. There is nothing that makes them feel uncomfortable, except that which is within their own self. There is no one there to cast them down and out. It is very soothing, for they will be harder on their own self than any of those with them could be. We are only judged by our own perceptions; we are always loved by those who we were taught would persecute us.

You see, when you are in that state of being, there is no judgment, no condemnation. At that moment of being, you are on a higher elevation of understanding so that it is impossible to be negative in any way or fashion. Yes, you will feel the pain of humiliation for your own actions, but not the type of pain you feel here. You will celebrate a jubilation of your accomplishments and then the awareness of your graduated elevation from their accomplishments.

I like to say it is like this: You have a contract; it is up to you how you write out your contract for this lifetime. Now, place yourself in a classroom with your peers among you. You have a teacher in front of the class with your homework assignment. You are allowed to choose which assignments you wish to follow, who you need and want to help you in your group and how you will do the assignment. All of you in your group sit down and discuss who will be doing what with the assignment, and when each one will do their part of the assignment to assist you along the way. The teacher then gives you the necessary tools and equipment. You place them all in your backpack. You open the door in front of you, and you step into the assignment – Mother Earth.

As we transition home, it is like opening that door back up from the other side and once again meeting up with all of those in your group to then discuss how the assignment went, what was learned and what was accomplished. You are among your own peers during this time; you remember back to when you were in your school classroom when you were asked to hand in your homework. What did you experience at that time? Did you have your homework done? Did you deserve an "A" for doing all that needed to be done? There is no difference to me in what is shown to me with each transition and what I experienced myself in my own near-death experience, for there is always Love.

Now from here, we look to what we could have done to change the outcome of anything that was not our best work, how we made the other individual feel as we did, what we thought we needed to do in that learning phase of our assignment or education and what could we have done to make a situation better than the way it turned out to be. We look at every individual's life that we were a part of and the effect our own decisions had in their life. It might have been when we complimented someone on their own accomplishments and how that made them a success at what they then went on to do in their life. It might have been that we were not as nice as we thought and how that hurt the individual, which then led them to not be as successful as what they could have been at that time or we held them up on their own life's path a little longer than it should have been.

After all of this is done, we then step away knowing that we have choices to make: we can choose the option of being born back to Mother Earth; we can choose to work with those who need more time acclimating; we can choose to work with children; or we can choose to be a guide in one way or another to another physical being on Mother Earth. We may choose to live a incarnation in another planetary solar system We have so many options open to us. We usually choose that which we have not accomplished yet. We then open the door and walk into the classroom to begin our next step of higher learning.

Many individuals hurt so much from their loved ones

transitioning; we all do but on different levels. It all depends on our own relationships that we had with our loved ones. I believe no two are alike. To this I say, be careful not to judge someone in their own grieving process as you do not know truthfully what hurt, pain or joy they hold close to them from their own relationship with their loved one. Also, I see those who are in so much pain from losing their loved ones that they cannot tear themselves away from the pain. I honor you, and my heart goes out to you – may you one day feel the love of the Christ in your heart once again.

I receive questions all the time from those who are in constant prayer to their loved ones and asking if this is hurting anyone in any way. Well yes, and no. No, because if it makes the physical individual feel peace or love in their heart, then it is good. And yes, as the physical individual is prolonging that which they really do not want to look at, including how the loved one has transitioned and that it is no one's fault. Also, this constant praying keeps their loved one who transitioned constantly busy trying to answer the phone calls they are receiving in the classroom. In other words, it is prolonging them from being able to go about the work they are doing.

Our loved ones know we are grieving and loving them at the same time. They will always be there when called; but remember, our loved ones see things on a whole different level, through a more pure view than we here have. They know that this is keeping us from our own path of learning. They try everything they can do to assist us along every step of the way.

This does not mean not to talk to them or ask them to be around. Oh yes, this is great; it is when we attach a lower denser energy to the request that keeps them from not moving along as quickly to graduate to a higher level of learning.

Chapter XIV

Contracts

You have read so much when I said our "Contracts" that I wanted now to explain what I am talking about. To me, we all have contracts that we have scripted before we are born here in this physical lifetime. Just as earlier when I talked about the classroom, if you noticed I mentioned we sit around and choose that which we want to learn and who we will work with to learn it.

This we do before we are born in each and every physical incarnation we choose to be a part of. We ask those loved ones around us to be a part of this physical experience, whether in the spiritual form as a guide, teacher, angelic guidance, or those who we ask to be with us in the physical body as our parents, siblings, friends, grandparents, associates, road blocks, karma busters, love interest and children born to us.

We start to map out that which each of us needs to learn during that time for our own life journey or life path, in our learning, development, growth and ascension. We take this time very seriously because with each one who will be with us either physically or spiritually, we will need to be there for each other in what the other needs to learn and process all that will go on and happen around them. A life map is mapped out in this process.

Now I want you to understand that when we are in this phase of mapping out our contracts we are not connected to emotional or physical feelings, society's dictates, pain, anger, thirst, hunger, hatred, etc. We are resonating and vibrating at a much higher frequency of love. We have no concept of what the emotional or physical demands may be. We know and are aware of what a physical person can do to one another; we know the places and events but not the emotional or physical sensations that are attached to it. We have no preoccupation with the physical demands of war from one human to another.

In whatever degree that the physical human can inflict something on another, it is not in us at that moment to feel or be a part of. We are mapping out our learning and experiences from a totally different perspective.

It will be up to the one who is with us physically or spiritually, as our spiritual guides and teachers or human guides and teachers, to come into our incarnated lives at the appointed times in accordance with our contract of our life journey or life path for the learning lessons we have already chosen to go through.

Now, if we get to a place of our life path/journey that we have not reached the learning lesson we have chosen to do, it is also up to our guides and teachers in spiritual and physical form to do what they can to get us back on our path. This can happen in so many ways, such as a near-death accident, or being involved with another individual, or changing jobs or going through the process of seeing a loved one transitioning, etc. I also like to remind my students and clients that as we grow in our own spiritual path of light and try to take short cuts along the way, if we do not listen to guidance that is being given to us, if we do not recognize the teachings that are given to us, if our own ego stands before us and we do not place it away, then we will be taken off our feet. In our contracts we have chosen for our spiritual and physical guides, angels, teachers, etc., to assist us in getting through all of these hurdles of this incarnated lifetime and more, but if at any time we are just ignoring the assistance and letting our ego, our own denial of who we are and what we are here to do, lead the way, then the universe will symbolically take us off our feet. I have had those who choose to ignore their guidance that they were receiving and letting their ego get in the way, and then their own life was falling in around them to one degree or another. I know many individuals who just keep making one excuse after another and still do not seem to get the bigger picture; to this day, they are still struggling. Then there are those who say, "Okay, okay ? I got it" and turn their whole lives around; they are prospering and manifesting like crazy.

I do not like telling others they will be knocked off their own feet, but if the message is there for me to give in this area, I will always do so. As a teacher it is my responsibility to assist in all ways given to me to guide those who are brought in my path of light from my own Counsel of One.

Then again, we did not consider "free will of choice" that we as humans have in this lifetime. Yes, it is your own choice which direction you take or which decisions you make. This planet of Mother Earth is far more accepting of this decision to be the holder of this free will of choice for the human race. But with choice comes the price to pay in our own lives, so we consciously make a choice to be all that we can and give in every way to one another because what is the result if we keep that which is to be given to us and hold onto it for our own gain? This is a choice we all need to think about.

Every contract that you have made, in every incarnation that you have chosen to make, takes you one step closer to that completion of who you are. In this contract you have made this lifetime, take time to look at what you believe you may have already written for your spiritual journey and all that it stands for and bring the Light of God into your own life to complete that which is before you in the purest of Love you may give to yourself and others.

Can contracts be changed? Yes, they can. You may change your contract at any time, and you do. Each moment of your life you are constantly changing that which you have written. Did you not write out a list of "to-do items" and did you do them? Or did you just keep looking at the list? With each step you take to fulfill your contract, you are adding that which is waiting for you to discover and your contract is opened and revealed to you more.

Everyone has "three outs" in this lifetime, meaning you have pre-chosen to have recorded in your contract three times in which you may leave this physical incarnation if things are not going according to your contract or if you have reached a level of learning where you have said that it is okay to leave after this or that level of accomplishment. These also may be times when we have experienced something major, such as a heart attack that we lived through, an accident where everyone tells you "you are lucky to be alive" or an illness or sickness where you have had an out-of-body or near-death experience. There are so many choices when it comes to these three outs and they are very serious; it means that you have pre-chosen to select events or time frames, not knowing what they may be, to take you back home without waiting for your "time." You already acknowledge at some moment in your life that things might get out of hand or be harder than you think they might be, and this would give you that which you need to either wake up, shake up, open yourself up more or go home with glory and dignity in every regard.

If then, you are so amazing in the spiritual form to have an awareness as to things that might come about and what you would need to survive this physical incarnation, then do you not see the true magnificence of who you are right now in this physical body? You have everything that you need to walk in the light of your own true divinity and to be that vehicle that can assist others in their own acclimation here on Mother Earth!

# Chapter XV

Religion and the Message

I just wanted to take a moment and try to give to you that which I have experienced and discovered in my many travels through the Universal Realms.

To me being Spiritual is not an organized religion in any way. We have all had one form of teachings from the variety of religious organizations in this life. And what a foundation that we have had because of this, good bad or indifferent. I say this, as we all need a foundation on which to build from. That is what this is all about foundations. And could you imagine what the world would be like if there was no organized religion at all? We think there is turmoil now within ourselves and the world.

I know there is intended for this world to have such structure; it is up to each living being in this world to serve that structure to the best of their ability. It is also to me, intended for those same said structures to then give to their parishes that which God has intended for them to give. Is it up to us then, to understand what God intended for us to know and give? I believe so, I believe that we are all responsible for doing what we know and feel deep inside of us and to stop placing the blame on something other than ourselves.

How many times does something go wrong in our lives that we then say "why God, why did this have to happen? Where are you when I need you?" But what most fail to see is that God is there for each of us in our moments of need. That is a promise that is within each of us. It is our own self which is the ego side, looking not to blame ourselves when this happens, but look to God to lay the blame. But God also says we must take the responsibility for our own actions. Is this not then where organized religion comes into play?

A place where we can go to commune with God in a community of like-minded individuals all seeking the answers to that which we do not know? Or, on the other hand, that which we do not want to take responsibility for? For when we do go to these structures, do they not have a symbolization of God there for us to look upon to receive that which we are seeking? That which we believe will fill us in such a way that we have the answers as long as we are there. Then there are those who believe they have found the answer and then lose it along the way to keep seeking it. One day it might make sense and fill the void, which is in us. For God says come to me and I shall give you that which you need. So, where is this place that we go to receive that which God has for us to receive? To most individuals it is a church or an organized religious structure for that is what society has raised us to believe. That we must seek out these structures for our own salvation.

I once meet a minister who I laid at his feet questions about getting in touch with God and why do I need to do this in a church structure, he looked at me and said "what you say is true you do not need a church to seek that which you need to receive. For you may talk to the Lord at any given time and place. What you need a church for is to gather together to worship in the Lords name as one". Now mind you , I had presented the same question to at least four different organized religions and all of them made me feel as I was dirt – unclean and unwashed and I would never be accepted into the house of God for my own belief structures in what I do. And if I did it would take years.

Now mind you, I was not seeking a church to begin with, I had been sent on a mission as a messenger. However, this one minister gave me the answer I was seeking, for as I was seeking out these answers I was also seeking them in the name of the Lord. I was a messenger. And as a messenger I was to find that house of God that truly spoke his word to their parishners. I was to find the one who had the spirit moving through them. I was to seek and learn what had been happening through all the time that we have lived here on Mother Earth and what kept happening over and over again as time went on. God's houses of worship was falling and I was sent to find out why.

I did go to this ministers church each week for worship they never asked anything of me, I sang the songs of old and let my voice be heard for the angels to sing with me, I sat and listened as the minister gave what was needed, and I watched them grow. And then one day I was lead to drop everything to go to this church, there it was, the change that I was to watch for. The church was growing and it was then being lead by the energy that had arrived. I was very cautious this day and then I found out why. As I sat there listening I heard the minister talk about authorities, and how no one has authority over another and then as I watched the minister speak I was warped front row center into a vortex of energy as the minister raised up books in front of himself and said to his parishners. " do not read this book, for in it the author says you may talk to God yourself, this author is touring the country telling our children how they could have conversations with God" I did not listen no more, I was so thrown back that these words were said. One minute about authority and no one telling you what to do and then the next minute bam, he too was telling individuals what to do. Now what kind of mixed signal is that?

I went home that day and sat in meditation with my Counsel and asked what just happened. I was told the time had come and there were going to be break downs in the organized religion as we know it , that the time had come for people to know the truths and the organized religions did not want the truth to be told. The energy was here to support all those who were called to the light. It was time for all Lightworkers to begin their awakening journey.

I never walked back into a church after that day of any

denomination as a place of personal worship. I know where I am to be. I know that we need a foundation of organized religion for individuals to have to build upon. For if we did not have that structured as a foundation in our lives, there would be panic and turmoil. There would be much misunderstandings. No one would know where to go to receive any type of solace, or to give out questions they needed answers to. To find the peace they had been trained to seek from these organized religions. For we as humans have not found truly how to process within our own self, we will always need something other than ourselves to be the one to blame.

But the time has come for us to go within and seek the answers we need, do we just cut out organized religion, well that my friend, is for you to find and discover for yourself. I am not here to tell you not to go to these organized structures of churches, as I have said before humankind has been trained through societies conditionings to seek the house of worship for their needs. And I am just a messenger for you to see that which is already before you, you just need to finally open your eyes to what was being played out. This does not mean that the churches cannot re-structure themselves to give what is actually needed and to stop with the fear that sometimes is at play for you then to come back to be saved.

I will say to you, the time has finally come to open everything up in a way of enlightenment. Since that time of authority was laid at the feet of all those individuals there that day. I have watched as I was told to do, all the years that have went by. How one after another of churches in all organized religion were having problems in one area or another. Their structures were being re-organized and re-built, the ego's run real high in these sections, they look for ways to bring in to add to their congregations but they then do not apply all that they teach. For if an organized religion actually gave the full truth to their work, they would have to answer questions they themselves are not ready to answer.

One day we will see these organized structures be bright and beautiful once more. We will see them give truths for all to have and then fill the need that is there, and in all of this these churches will find the answer of truths that everyone seeks was not hidden at all, it was with them as God is with them. God is just waiting for them to seek what shall be given, knock and the door shall be open, ask and you shall receive. I Bless them all and I look forward to the day when we shall all have true peace within our hearts to give to one another across the miles.

Now in all of this I want to ask you about your own spiritual awakening. When did you feel it? What was going on in your life? How did you know you were having a spiritual awakening? In addition, exactly who are you? Right now right this minute who are you? Just sit here and take a moment and ask yourself, take a nice deep breath and relax . Now then, look within and take the time to know yourself. Go ahead, I shall wait.

Tell me what did you find? Did you find you are seeking something within you that is asking for more? Did you find that you are so tired of seeking and not getting anywhere? Did you just have a moment in time when something one day just click? Have you been apart of an organized religion all of your life or part of your life when something seemed missing? Or one day were you sitting in church and just knew you needed to finally hear the truth. And here is a big one. Did one day you learn so much from all sectors of your religion that you touched the hand of God and just knew you where here to do something awesome, a mission?

Then welcome to Spirituality! Might I say does it not

feel wonderful? I love knowing that I can commune with God and have God with me and know that God is there. My faith is what is so strong that no one can diminish it in any way. I can knowingly tell you straight up this each time you ask. You will never hear me say I do not believe.

WHO IS JESUS

Three key words; BELIEVE, TRUST, FAITH and LOVE

Love is not a key word Love just is. Love is something that we as a spiritual individual has that emanates from us. Love is God. Love is the key to all keys.

Let me tell you about a man who was raised fully open. He was born to a humble family who believed they would always be provided for. The family took that trust and sent their son to a place of learning. One for him to understand their religious belief structure and grow in the words of God. This took the boy on amazing journeys of understanding and fulfillment. The boy would go and question his elders and seek until he found there was no one who could answer him, so he then sat down, taught and gave them answers that they were seeking. As this boy journeyed along the way he grew in his own relationship with God. He found that he was connected to something so amazing – God. He went back to his humble home and sought counsel with his family. He shared his journeys as they sat and recognized him for the young man he had grown to be. As his time of sharing came to an end with his family, he then took himself out into the world. He was being led by faith to find that which he was seeking, as he had been told to do.

He then found himself by a river where his own cousin came to him and said " It is I who shall cleanse and should baptize you". He allowed his cousin to lead him into the waters to be cleansed to be given the light of God onto his body and be anointed for all to see to make him whole. As it so happened, he was being baptized and cleansed of all impurities he had to give over to God. He was saying into your God I give my being in which I am. He laid down all of his transgression, he was asking to be cleansed, healed and made whole to receive that which God had for him. And in that moment of complete surrender of all things unclean and unholy God opened the heavens and said for all to hear, "behold this is my son, for in him I am most pleased."

The light that shined out was so bright that others could not look, the music from the heavenly angels was so pure and loving no one could hear, for they themselves where not cleansed to receive this blessing. But at that moment in time they all saw this young man become a vessel of such pure light energy from God, they bowed down and prayed. They too then went into the river to be made clean and whole.

That man then raised himself out of the river and walked in the light of God. For God was leading him to be where he was needed. He did what he had been asked by God to do. To minister to God's children. To gather all that he needed to do his work and as long as he was in the truths of what God had given him, he shall always be with God.

To this day, everyone knows one story or another about this man. For he was just that, a man. A physical man who had a spiritual awakening and knew he had a mission to fulfill. So, I ask you who are you? Are you not a physical person having a spiritual awakening? Was not Jesus a physical man having a spiritual awakening? Did not Jesus say "for these things I do you shall do greater?" Do you understand that which Jesus was giving to you, when he said this? To learn and do as he had done, and then go out and do greater things? How easy is that?

Remember the time when Jesus went into the desert, with nothing but his own self. He had to face many negative things, he had to learn how to have trust of what was being given to him, but he also had to process that which he was holding onto in his physical body. He was being called by something larger to look at and to understand his role in all of it. He was facing his own spiritual awakening and needed to process what that meant and what he needed to release from his mind, body and spirit, to then be open to receive Gods true messages for him. Messages that were not attached to ego or the negative. He needed it to be known to himself that everything he received was coming from God and nothing else. He waited for his guidance to come and when it did, Jesus was put through the challenge of recognizing what was before him. He then had to go within to see the truth of all situations all issues and all resentments that he had been holding onto in his body, mind and spirit for so long. The belief structures which he was raised in, the equations which made him who was at that moment in time. He was to be given many visions and as these visions came up before him, he had to deal with them in a truthful way and lay them to rest. He demonstrated his faith in God by doing this, he was given many visions of things that had happened and had past. In addition, he was asked to seek the truth in all of it. Then he was asked to forgive, to forgive all before him, to forgive from his inner soul and trust what God was giving to him. Most importantly, he was asked to forgive himself in all transgression that he had held onto for so long.

Jesus was tired, emotional and drained from this experience as he was going though it, he would question those things which came up, we was being challenged to give everything he had to God. To trust God in such a way as he had not recognized before. And as he was going through all of it, he knew deep inside his soul that what was being given to him was truth. He could not understand why this was being given to him now, when it had not been given before. Why was he not told the truth from the very beginning of what he was learning and knew to be truth? He like you, knew from the beginning he was hearing the truth, but did not realize till then it was the truths that was given by humankind not by the power and authority of God.

Jesus walked out of the desert enlightened in a way that no humankind could touch him again. He was living the truth of God and he was there to bring the truth of Gods words to humankind.

Is Jesus' work and words, not that of God. Did Jesus not leave us the blueprint in which we are to grow in Gods work and words? Did not Jesus leave us that which we need to grow in our own enlightment and do greater work than he?

Just as you will be doing as you process all of your fears, resentment and issues this is the same as Jesus was doing. As a physical man, Jesus had the same temptations that you face in your own life. He knew in order to be welcomed into the kingdom of God, to be apart of his mission here he had to have enough faith and trust in the one who called to him. God. Jesus needed to take that which was holding him fully back from his true mission here on Mother Earth, out of his body so that when he ascended he was a clean, clear and pure vehicle. He was the true son of God in everyway. He was going to be that which he knew he was to be. A messenger in Gods army of Light. To give the ultimate of sacrifices to then give to others.

Jesus needed to take anything that was negative in his life and body and be rid of it, he need this time to process and ask for a pure mind, body and soul. Is this not what you are doing?

Jesus needed to cleanse himself of all earthly desires, for what is in an earthly desire that really gives us truth in which we will have to take with us? There is nothing to take to the kingdom of God, that God needs as much as God needs for you to have the faith that everything you need you shall have in God. For you are a divided aspect of God. In saying this what is it that God needs of you?

When I was asked by the Blessed Mother to teach that which I had been learning since I was a small child. I was honored and then frightened, as to what it would be. Who am I to have these teachings to then give to others? Is this not a question you ask yourself each day? And then the Blessed

Mother said, "my son took that which was given to him and ask these same things, he journeyed to the mountains and would question it himself. And he learned and went through that which he needed to do Gods work, so to shall you."

I had to stand back and to me, process and think about what all of this meant. This was such a huge responsibility; I was not the perfect person in Gods eyes to do all of this. I had my own trials along the way in my life. But I knew I trusted God in all that I do. As I took the time to think on all that was before me, it was not long before I too was going through the same as Jesus. I did not go to the mountains or deserts, I was in a hit and run car accident.

That was the beginning to everything before me. When my car was hit from behind, I had looked up and not seeing what was coming I instead saw a bright white light and then bam, I was sitting beside Jesus up in the mountains so high it was beautiful. We were sitting there talking about the world when I looked over and said, "oh my goodness, what am I doing here right now, when last we talked like this I was preparing for my journey to Mother Earth and was getting my last look at what I was to be doing in my earthly life mission".

It was the most surreal moment of my life, I was actually sitting with Jesus and knowing that I was not ready to be here in that moment of time as I was still in a earthly body.

Jesus looked at me and said, "do you think you have ever left my side?" I looked at him and said, "no, but I do know that from the time of this talk with you, I had left for Mother Earth and about my business of going to my earthly home to my husband and children after a long day of work." Jesus smiled and said, " Did not mother let you know it was time to do the work you had contracted to do with your journey to Earth?" I sat there and looked back over the mountain, taking all of its beauty in and said "yes, I am having a few problems there, you know the life I lead on earth while in human form, you know that I have had many challenges along the way, I am not accepted for what I know or who I am". Jesus sat there and said "was I accepted also as you would like to be?, did I not give all of what I was to then bring Gods words to humankind?" I looked into the bluest of eyes and knew he spoke the truth for me to see once again all that we have been and will always be, we are here to bring Gods Children into the Light of their own knowing. A knowledge of completion of our learning to an accelerated degree.

We sat there side by side and I asked Jesus about my children, what would their lives be if I decided to just stayed home with him, I was starting to acclimate and find who I was again in his presence. He talked about what they would accomplish with their own contracts of learning and how the loss of me in their own lives, would in this critical area be sorely tested for each of them. And if I do choose to stay that he would then allow me to assist another in fulfilling the prophecy of their own mission. For I knew in that moment of time everything I am and have ever been in each lifetime that I had chosen to procreate as a living being on Mother Earth.

I sat there and gave Jesus a large hug and said "I choose to go back to my family on Mother Earth and fulfill my mission to teach as many Children of God the way to the New Jerusalem" and at that moment I was flying above my vehicle, I could see all of the traffic around it and then I could hear a car horn blowing and at that moment I saw an impact from behind my vehicle, I saw the car in which hit my own, back up. And then I was there looking into the window of the person who had hit my vehicle. And I only saw darkness in the place of where the face was to be. I walked away and looked at myself sitting behind the wheel with my head up against the steering wheel. Then I was in my own body. I could feel nothing but confusion on what just happened as this woman was coming to my window telling me I hit her. I heard a car horn and a car zoom around us both as if getting away. I then looked behind me and no one was there, no car nothing.

I could see the firehouse sitting across from us with firefighters outside but no one was looking, everyone was going about their own time as if nothing was happening here. I got out of my vehicle and told the woman how sorry I was, I did not remember hitting her and there was still the same amount of space left between our vehicles as when I had pulled up behind her. How could I have hit her? I took responsibility at that moment as I heard a child crying, I asked the mother if her child was okay and she seemed not to be concerned about her child as she said her child was okay. As we left there, I remembered that never in my whole life had I been in an accident and I did not still understand how I had hit this woman's vehicle as there still had been space enough for two cars between us and she had not been knocked into the traffic at the light. So then I had to understand and see as how she too, was apart of this contract for me to decide if I was ready or not to do Gods work.

After much physical work on my mind and body from the repercussions of the trauma my body had sustained from the hit and run accident. The doctors told me there was not much more they could help me with. I had no coherent thought process, my speech was barely audible in making sense in what I wanted to say, my body hurt all over and I had had a concussion and black eye. I still had not chosen to do my work, and as a weekend came along I was cooking on the grill out back of my home. I was going down the steps when I started to fall side ways. As I was falling, my whole foot gave way and it was pulled and twisted back in the opposite direction. I could not move I sat there and started crying form the pain, my foot could not be touched or moved and I definitely could not walk on it. After being transported to the hospital I was placed in a non-walking cast for nine months.

Do you see that? A non-walking cast. I was being told I was not going to be doing anything else until I did my work because this was very important.

I got it and I will do it. This started me on a year long journey where I had to go within and process everything before me. It was just as Jesus had done, and on top of it all I had to teach myself once more how to read, write and speak . It was one of the hardest things to go through for my family, I would forget things and I could not talk right for them to understand me. I was given the biggest challenges of my life at that moment and I had to do it for all of us.

The Blessed Mother was there the whole time, she came to me and would teach me even more of what the process was all about as I was going through it. How what I needed to look at and see it for the truth of what it really was. How as we do this we are going to be emotional we are creating the truth of our world. Our whole life structure needs to be taken apart and re-assembled in the truth of the Light of Gods words. To go through everything that we had been conditioned to accept as the truth and to see the calculations of what the differences are between truth and un-truths. I was now physically going through what Jesus had gone through in his own physical life here on Mother Earth.

As I was nearing the end of the year, I was on my front porch pouring out the rest of it giving God everything I had all my love, trust and faith and then I heard the Blessed Mother whisper in my ear. Go ahead, go and get your camera, be ready.

I did just that and as I was finishing all of my gratitude, giving my life to God and the will of God, I was enveloped in the most brilliant and amazing light, I was being drawn up into the Love that is God, I could feel my whole body come alive and I was crying for the re-union of Gods love. The heavens were opening me , welcoming me and baptizing me in Gods love. The Holy Spirit was descending upon me and I was in a state of something so pure it is indescribable. And then I remembered my camera and took pictures of everything. The Blessed Mother told me this was my gift from God to give and show others so that they may too see that which God has promised them. I was enveloped in this pure loving energy for so long that I did not want it to end.

Afterwards my husband came to the door, he had seen something and saw me crying and wanted to make sure I was okay. I could feel the light emanating around and through me and I just laughed. Here I was given the most precious gift we as humans can have and there was nothing earthly that could touch me any more. For the Holy Spirit Had descended on me, I had touched the light of God and my place in this lifetime was sealed and secured. I am here as a messenger and I am here as God messenger. Everything that I will ever need is before me. For everything I need is God.

I ran in and downloaded the picture I was given and it is magnificent, there is much to see all through it. I was told by the Blessed Mother, that when one looks upon this picture it is for them to see the truths of God. And each will see something another does not. This gift is a gift of the Holy Spirit and miraculous things shall come to all who gaze upon it.

If you would like a copy of this amazing picture, please just send me a note in a self addressed stamped envelope in a 11 x 14 size, and I will send it to you.

What I went through and experienced in what the Blessed Mother placed in my hands the alchemical equation for all of God's children to ascend into the light of God. To be just like Jesus in being baptized and having the heavens open up above and God saying to you as to Jesus "behold this is my son, for in him I am most pleased". As you apply all that I am teaching you in this book and you apply all of it into your life, you will have God's energy descend upon you and you will feel the most precious of love that there is. It will be so beyond description, but in that moment of time you will know it and you will feel exactly why you are here on Mother Earth and what you are seeking. This I promise you.

Being spiritual is about love. Opening yourself to a higher level of energy, to acknowledge that which is in each and everyone of us. And knowing that we are all one with the Divine. And that as we go through all of this in this lifetime that the Divine is always with you. To give the love that we all so seek in ourselves and one another.

In all that I leave you, I leave you my story of ascension, the day I sat beside Jesus and was given the answer to that which I was seeking.

Chapter XVI

Cleansing and Clearing

I could not end this book without adding this very important area that needs to be added into our lives on a daily basis as we move forward in who we are. It is a most important chapter as with everything we do we need that which we sometimes overlook.

The work that I am giving you in this chapter is one that I give and teach to all of my students as they begin to work with me, whether you want to be a teacher, healer, medium, psychic or to assist you in your spiritual well-being. These are visualizations to cleanse yourself on a daily basis. As I have talked about before in the previous chapter of cleansing and clearing oneself, this to me as you have read is very important part of who we are on many levels in what we do and who we are. In this line of work and with any form of work you do on a daily basis, you are continuously slammed with people dumping on you twenty-four seven.

When I say dumping I mean people who you come in contact with each day who are always giving you their own stuff. This stuff is that which is bothering them and they need to talk about it or share with someone else to get a better understanding of everything. This stuff is what someone has been collecting all day at work or when they have just gone through a situation and need to tell or share the situation with someone else to help alleviate their own minds. When your girlfriend calls you up with her problems she is having with her spouse, work, partner or another friend, she is seeking you out to talk everything over with you. She is asking you to be the vehicle to listen as she pours out her heart and frustrations , you listen and give her the shoulder she needs to lean on . This is called dumping. There is no problem here with being the loyal friend, it is when this is going on, when that connection is being made to listen to what is being said to you and you are now taking on all that she is saying you are actually allowing yourself to be dumped on.

This is what it looks like, as your friend is alleviating herself of all her frustrations, and troubles to you, that energy of whatever the situation may be is being poured over you like sludge of mud. In addition, as your day goes along you are constantly having more mud poured over you from each individual you meet who seeks you out for being the vehicle to listen with an open heart and mind. Which brings you at the end of your day fully covered from head to toe with this huge sludge of mud on your energy body. So instead of your energy and aura being bright and beautiful, it is dull and tired and weighing you down. This causes so many to be exhausted, uninterested, drained, worn-out, developing the signs of stress and depression along the way. Which ends up over time of not being able to focus and be clear to proceed with what your really want to go out and do.

This also leads to being a vehicle that is not cleansed and clear, so that when you then do your work as a healer, psychic, medium, teacher or a lightworker, you are transferring that energy to others. Think about it, if I let myself go all day working with individuals and not clearing and cleansing my own self, I am then going to be sending this same form of energy to others that I work with. This is not fair to the other when they have their own stuff to deal with, so as I work with the individual they are not only receiving the energy I am calling in to assist them they are also receiving the energy left over from someone else, they then have a compounded amount of energy to have to deal with which is not all theirs. Another way we look at this is, when we walk into the front door of your home, what do you feel ? Does it feel fresh and ready as you walk through the door to start whatever you have on your mind, or is it a little sluggish and you then just sit down to relax and sometimes feel tired or saddened ? This is the residuals from the energy that you have been bringing in and out of your home each day. The extra sludge that then leaves its imprint on the areas in which you live. When you apply the clearing methods I have for you, you will start to feel the freshness once again as you are welcomed home each day.

We are constantly being taught that we need to cleanse and clear ourselves and our homes, but so many believe they do not need it for one reason or another or just plain forget to do so. Moreover, after a length of time, they then wear themselves down and have no clue as to what is going on. Their energy is low or different and they start to share their own frustrations with others and then the whole cycle is repeated from person to person all over again.

All that it takes is to be focused and disciplined in who we are and the amount of work we are doing to get a routine established, once this is done it will then be such a part of your life that you will not want to live without it and you will greatly noticed when you do not do it on a regular basis. Here are a few simple ways in which to cleanse and clear yourself.

To Cleanse and Clear in the Shower or Bathtub

When you are finishing your shower or bath and rinsing your body off, just visualize yourself standing right in front of you. Almost as if there was a paper cut out of yourself standing there before your eyes. You may close your eyes to do so, which makes it much more complete as this will help with the focus as you start to discipline yourself. You may see this as an outline of the physical body, you may be as large or small as you want. Sometimes I see myself three inches long, sometimes two feet tall , there is no wrong size or way to do this. Now take a look at your energy field around your body. How does it look, how does it feel? Is it large or small, is your energy field thick or thin and do you see any specific color or shape to it? Now you may feel this or see it, both are okay and it will take you time to practice this, so if you at first feel or see as if there is nothing there do not worry, the more you do this the stronger it will get. It is all about focus, intention and discipline. This is called learning the intent of visualizations. The more you work on developing it the more you will start to see or feel it.

As you are seeing yourself in front of you as a whole being or an outline, I want you to see a golden light rod horizontally on the top of where the head is (remember this is the top of your head you have projected in front of you) now take your hand and move this golden light rod down your body repeating these words:

I cleanse and clear myself now of all negativity, fear, evil and harm

Making sure you bring this golden light rod down your whole body until everything that you are cleansing goes into the drain beneath your feet. Feel all the sludge of mud from your energy field flowing down your body being washed away into the drain beneath your feet.

Now bring the golden light rod back up to the top of the head once more and say these words:

I cleanse and clear myself now of all anger, jealousy, judgment and self-judgment

Feel all the sludge of mud from your energy field flowing down your body being washed away into the drain beneath your feet. As you bring the golden rod down your body.

Now bring the golden light rod back up to the top of the head once more and say these words:

I cleanse and clear myself now of all stress, anxiety, depression and illness.

Now as you are doing this you can feel and see all of this sludge of mud moving down your body and entering in the drain of your shower or bathtub, feel how much lighter you feel, how much your energy vibration is picking up and shining out. You may continue with this process of focusing and cleansing, as you will know there are other things you wished to be cleared of. Anything that has come up in your day that you want taken way with this golden rod to cleanse and clear yourself with, add it to the cleansing and clearing. Go ahead and add it, I look at it this way if I am thinking about it then I am going to wash it away. When you are finished with this and you have nothing else that comes to mind to cleanse, go ahead and see all of it going into the drain beneath your feet and say:

Mother Earth I ask you to take all of this that I cleanse and clear from my body now and absorb it into your body, Transmute and transform this into Love, light, laughter, peace, sharing, caring, friendship, and return it to the Universe to all living beings. As you say this, once again you may add anything else that comes to your mind that you would like to lovingly share with others. And, as you release this energy see it swirl around you and go up into the Universe. Remember Mother Earth will take all that you give her and then transmute it and transform it to what you then ask of her. This is also saying you do not wish for her to keep it herself to work on later. We give enough to Mother Earth for her to process and never ask her to send it back. This way you are asking for her assistance and then asking her to re-send the transformed energy back to the Universe to be dispensed to all living beings, this is why I say "you would like to lovingly share with others." This is all about cleansing, clearing and healing, it is all done in Love.

You are now cleansed, cleared and ready to go. Take a moment to breath in the freshness that is now you, feel it and know this is what you feel like all cleansed cleared and ready for anything. I always end it with a lovely prayer of Light Protection such as this one that has been around for so long, you may find it on the internet at anytime.

The Light of God

The Light of God surrounds me
The Love of God enfolds me
The Power of God protects me
The Presence of God watches over me
Wherever I am God Is
So be it, Amen

This lovely prayer may be used as many times a day and at anytime of the day to bring that energy of God, a peaceful loving strong energy of God all around you.

Now what about during the day or night when the shower or bath is not an option, well as long as you are doing your daily cleansing it is okay to go to the bathroom and as you are washing your hands cleanse and clear the same way as if you wherein your shower or bath. This is a good cleansing when you are at work and need to be cleansed and cleared or in-between working with clients, after you have been out shopping especially during the holidays. Remember there are many forms of cleansing and clearing, I have given you just an example of one that is very powerful and works to cleanse and clear you.

Now I would like to share with you three cleansing, clearing and protection Prayers that were channeled to me by Archangel Michael may many years ago and he has given these to me to share with others. These prayers are very powerful and do exactly as you ask, you will notice a difference in your home, car and work environment immediately. I always give these to my students when the first begin to work with me and they will all tell you how these three seemingly simple prayers have changed their lives for the positive and assisted them in taking away the fears that they had been holding onto for a very long time. These are not just clearing, cleansing and protection prayers, Archangel Michael likes to say they are Empowering prayers from him to you. With these prayers you may start to use them as soon as you like, when you are first starting to use them apply all three in sequence one right after the other. At first, you might like to say them morning, noon and night. That is greatest as with each time you do say them the energy gets stronger and stronger. You will notice how you can recite these prayers without even thinking about it and the wonderful news is as you do Archangel Michael is right there, to assist you. Once you start to focus and discipline yourself with reciting these lovely powerful prayers you will notice in a case of emergency the first thing out of your mouth will be prayers. It will not even be a thought to try to remember them. Remember they are every powerful and Archangel Michael will be right there!

Another important note is to remember that when we negate any prayer or any words and manifestations we send to the Universe and those in the Spiritual Realms to assist and guide us with, we then cancel out that which we are requesting their assistance for. It's like saying "I love You" and then turning right back around and saying "well, maybe I do". As soon as you send it out, KNOW that the Universe and all those in the Spiritual Realms are there beside you and are assisting you in every way. And the most important factor is one in which should not have to be said; THANK YOU. A thank you to everything you request of those in the Universe and Spiritual Realms goes a long way.

Enjoy and please let me know about your experiences as

you work with the cleansing and clearing exercises and these amazing powerful prayers.

Archangel Michael Prayer

Dear Archangel Michael, I ask for your assistance please
Dear Michael I ask you to go thru my <u>home</u> (car or place of work) from top to bottom
Inside and out, in every space, area, nook and cranny and room,
And clear out all negative earth bound entities
All earth bound entities, all negative entities,
All negativity, evil, fear, harm, judgment, jealousy, etc..
(add anything else you would like)
And sweep it up into the white light of the Holy Spirit
Thank you Michael,   Amen

Mother Father God

Dear Heavenly Mother Father God,
please send your loving Angels
One million strong into my home, from top to bottom
Inside and out, in every space, area, nook and cranny
and room, that Michael has just cleared.
May they radiate your love and illuminate your light
As they sing your praise and glory.
Thank You , Amen

Archangel Michael Please

Archangel Michael I ask for your assistance once again
I ask you Michael and your Band of Mercy, to please
surround my home from top to bottom , inside and out and
ask that you post your heavenly Angelic Guards
At every window, doorway and entryway and allow nothing
but those through the
Light and Love of the Holy Spirit to enter.
Thank you Dear Michael, Amen

Chapter XVII

Words to leave you by

As I end this book, I want to leave you with my Blessings for your own journey along your spiritual path of enlightenment. This lifetime, in which you have chose to be here right now, is by no accident, as I am sure you have heard this before. If not, I am honored to be the first to say these words to you. You are beautiful in the eyes of those around you and when you look in the mirror each day, please take the time to acknowledge how much you love yourself, for in loving your own self you then love God, for God is in you and with you each moment of your life. May you always feel the warmth & Love of gratitude as you humbly acknowledge these words.

In writing this book I wanted you the reader to see, sense, feel and know that with everything I am sharing with you is that which you already have within you to acknowledge. I give you my experiences my knowledge for you to identify your own self with. To grow and be that which you are here and meant to be. And for you to reconnect with what you have already experienced yourself, your own treasure of knowledge of the Spiritual Realms around you, whether by personal experience or from other individuals you have known as you have grown in this life. A chance for you to know that you are beautiful just as you are and yes, you are not alone in this world. We are all one; we are all the same, seeking that which always seems just out of reach. Now you have the tools to work with, It is a start in building your foundation for you to stand upon. Now let's begin to build the next levels of your foundation and ascend to be all that you are here to be.

I love this life of who I am, who I allow myself to be as I face the society in which I choose to be a part of, at this time in humankind's history. I thank each one of you for meeting me once again as we move forward to finish that which we choose to be a part of in this lifetime. I acknowledge the blessings each day that are laid at my feet and I acknowledge that you are part of those blessings. May you always see the beauty in who you are as you claim that which is you, that which is your Birth Right! I know as you have been reading pages that you are finding your own self-recognition, clarity and self-worth in the truths of these words. I am so happy to be of assistance to you along the way.

As we move along in the next few years we are going to be going through the cycle in which all of us has waited and prayed for: a re-newel and cleansing of body, mind, soul of Mother Earth and all who live upon her. A time of true inner knowing and peace "across the miles" from one heart to another. I have been given and shown much in this lifetime from the Universe and my own Counsel of One. My love and faith for God is never wavering, and so too, is tapping into that which is who I truly am. But never has it been more revealing and urgent than now, in this time that we all come together and work with our own selves and others to grow in our enlightenment as we move forward in this evolution of humankind. Take the steps before you to accomplish all of your goals, desires and learning, for you will be called upon from the highest of highs to walk the destiny of your own manifestations. We are at a time of such a huge explosion of Spiritual Evolution for all the reasons in which your heart cries each day. We are all here seeking the truths to live by. Open your heart to know you are not alone in who you are and what you are here to do. We are all here together at this time seeking a change in our own truths. Love just Love, a Love so pure your heart longs for. We are all here seeking Love.

I look forward to bringing you my next books, *"A Message is Just a Memory"* and *" It is Not my Message to Deliver"*, you can also look for my guided meditation CD's, to help you in your meditation work. May you always be blessed with Love.

Love, Laughter & Light, Adele

Adele's Meditation CD's:

These guided Meditations CDs are a part of my Development Classes that I teach on a weekly basis. I wanted to open that door for you to have a part of that teaching from across the miles to assist and guide you in your own development.

I will take you straight into a Guided Meditation that is being channeled to me as I speak the words to you, my own Counsel of One is showing and guiding me. As you listen to my voice I am taking you to the Realms in which to meet those of your own Counsel.

Each CD is an hour in length, with two thirty minute or more guided meditations, please be aware each guided meditation is to be done separately, allowing yourself to have the time in between meeting each of your own guides, angels and teachers, to truly get to know them. These CDs are a door opener to your own connection and relationship with each one.

Understand these are not all of your guides, angels and teachers in the spiritual realms, but just a few of the major ones whom you will get to know and work with on a daily basis. As time goes on, I will be introducing you to even more of your own Counsel who are with you each day.

I will be channeling more guided meditation CDs, but as always, I will be presenting some guided meditations that have never been heard before at my workshops, seminars and events, as these will be the ones that are given to me by my own Counsel, to bless, open up and connect with those who are attending these events.

You will be amazed as you find yourself actually meeting each of your guides, angels and teachers in the Spiritual Realms with these Guided Meditation CDs, the Joy, Love and knowledge that comes from them to you, and the recognition to each one in which you are about to meet. I send you my Blessings, and Love!

Love, Laughter & Light, Adele

Guided Meditation CD's

I want to give you these pages for you to have the chance to read what my meditations are all about. As we open ourselves up in this work, we are then opening ourselves up to the connection we have with all of our guides and teachers and a few in which I introduced you to earlier in this book. Take your time and enjoy as I hope you will find yourself understanding a little more on the ease on which it is to meet and work with our guides in the Spiritual Realms.

Counsel of One

It was easy for me to see the order in which these meditation CD's were to be offered to you. As in all things, the two guides who most influence us with their presence when we first start learning who is with us in our own Counsel is; our Joy Guide and Protector Guide. These two you will recognize as you get to meet them through your journey in this first CD- **"Counsel of One."**

Let me introduce a little about them now:

The Joy Guide

Children are impish and mischievous as a rule. The Joy Guide most often appears as a child, a small fairy like child and/or young maidenly adolescent. They can display behavior that would be described as mischievous. Your Joy Guide is the one who is responsible for bringing out the lighter side of our personalities. When things become missing, your Joy Guide is there to let you know to lighten it up. Even though your Joy Guide appears to be childish in many ways, be respectful to them, for your Joy Guide is highly intelligent in all ways as with all of your guides. When mirth and merriment manifest within a group of people unexpectedly for no particular reason, it is frequently the presence of someone's Joy Guide causing the frivolity and trying to get your attention. We could all certainly benefit from less stress by viewing some matters with a sense of humor.

Call upon your Joy Guide when your daily life becomes overwhelming, and you need to laugh aloud. Your Joy Guide will show you the humor in the situation. This Joy Guide is sometimes referred to as a Medium's "message bearer "and to help control the spirit crowd of an individual who is seeking a reading or channeling. Your Joy Guide my sometimes call you "Mommy" as she is of that child like energy, and wanting to make you happy and joyful.

I work with my Joy guide in all of my deliverance of messages as she controls the crowd in spirit and let them know what my "rules" are when I work. In my workshops and classes, she gathers other joy guides together to keep them busy and give them the outline of what we will be doing. Together then, they all come together to bring a lightness of energy when we need it, she is also my "hostess with the mostess" as she welcomes all who enter our home and greets everyone's guides, angels teachers and loved ones in spirit from the light, letting them know what is going on and who needs to do what.

The Protector Guide

The Protector Guide or your Native American Indian seems to be the guide everyone is most familiar with and expects to work with and hear from when in a private session with a medium. Since the Native American Indian is the true native of the United States, the Native American Indian appears most often. As I have said before, I have a friend who has a female Protector Guide with her and she looks like "Zena" a female warrior from the 1700's. More likely than not, you will have a Native American Indian, if you are from Africa, you might have one who looks like an African Warrior, from Sweden, you might have one who looks like a Viking. So, be relaxed and take what your guide shows you.

Your Protector Guide is usually the first one to make a strong presence with you, as you are more comfortable with their protective nature spirit. I have found that most Protector Guides work with those who are balanced and work with mother earth in one way or another, from the everyday yard work, to planting and working with herbs. Go ahead and work with the soil of mother earth, go to an area that has a small pond, stream or lake and get to know the area. Take notice of the plants in your yard and neighborhood, as you do so you will notice your Protector Guide presence around you and then as you are examining the local plants, you will start to understand all about the plants; you will find yourself thirsting for that knowledge to know more. This is the influence of your Protector Guide.

Many people feel the presence of their Protector Guide sitting next to them in a car when they travel, and some tell stories about accidents being averted due to their Indian guides. My Protector Guide is my first and most trusted best friend, who never leaves my side and always looks out for my best interest in my work, and when I lay down to go to sleep at night. I ask him to be at my side and watch over me as I sleep and dream, that no harm comes to me.

Counsel at Birth

As we grow in our awareness the next two guides are ones that everyone asks about the most and that there is much confusion over. We are living in the times when there is so much information on the World Wide Web, and it is wonderful to have all of that at your fingertips. So here too, is my take on what has always been shown to me and to what I know from the Universe of All.

As I introduce to you in the next CD **"Counsel at Birth"** we all have two guides from the time we are born here in this physical lifetime to the time when we transition home, and those two are your Guardian Angel and Your Gatekeeper Guide. They are not to be confused with one another or anyone else. Most of your other guides will stay with you for many years as you grow in your learning, when you have accomplished that which you need to move on - your guides celebrate with you and then it is time for them to bow out as your next guide or teacher comes in to work with you. So, let's meet them:

The Gatekeeper

The first guide in the band is called Gatekeeper, or Doorkeeper. I say this as the Gatekeeper is one of only two of your guides who are with you from birth to transition.

This beloved guide is one of my much loved guides (as they all are) one who works so close to me as this one does. Your gatekeeper is the guide who gives his consent or non-consent to the visiting clients - guides, teachers and loved ones in spirit, to communicate in a reading with the medium or yourself as the practicing medium.

Your Gatekeeper is with you from birth until you make your transition home, just as your guardian angel does, but please do not confuse the two of them, for they are totally different. This spirit guide is your overall protector in your life work and what you are here to do. The Gatekeeper looks over and watches out for your best interest and holds you close so no harm may come to you. Very often, when you see a Gatekeeper Guide around someone, the guide will stand behind or in front of that person, wearing a voluminous cape, with lots of enveloping folds. Which then, this guide will wrap the cape around the individual, which automatically signals a feeling of protection and identifies the guide as a Gatekeeper. You will also find the Gatekeeper will have characteristics similar to your own or a feeling of familiarity as with a past life.

Your Gatekeeper is the guide that is assisting you and a chosen reader when you have decided to receive a personal reading from a medium. The Gatekeeper's influence in this area is to make sure you are receiving the messages that you are there to receive.

Guardian Angels

Are Guardian Angels the same as a Spirit Guide or Teacher Guide? Well, Guardian Angels and Angels are spiritual beings who are very present in our lives and in a class all by themselves. What makes them angelic is that they have never incarnated on Mother Earth, unlike our Spirit Guides and teachers.

Our personal Guardian Angel is with us from birth until we make our transition home, as is our Gatekeeper - once again not to be confused with each other. Our Guardian Angel has never had a physical incarnation, while our Gatekeeper guides and teachers have had many a lifetime in physical form.

Our guardian angels are with us to keep us on our path of light, that when we may - by "free will of choice" wander away from our true divine path, then the guardian angel will guide us back to where we need to be. When you are in a harmful situation that can cause you to transition before your time, it will be your guardian angel who yells out very audibly to you "NO" or "Do not go there, turn back." This is such a strong and commanding voice that you will hear it, outside your body, next to you, that it will make you jump or stop in your tracks; listen to what your Guardian Angel says and do it right away!

Coming Soon
Counsel of Degree

The Next Guided Meditation CD will introduce your Doctor Teacher and Master Teacher to you in **"Counsel of Degree"** and these two guides have all the degrees they need as you step into meeting them.

The Doctor Guide

The Doctor Guide, also referred to as the physician, MD, medical, psychologist, therapist, is most prominent in a person's life when they work in a healing professional, such as a doctor, nurse, veterinarian, minister or spiritual healer. But not always limited to these responsibilities, you may at any one time have anywhere from one to four doctor guides or more, depending on what is going on in your life. Many of physical mediums have their Doctor Guide as their main guide in their work. Also, Doctor Guides are not limited to those in the medical profession as many doctor guides do not have a medical degree from in their many incarnated lifetimes, but have the doctor degree for the amount of work that they have achieved in all of their lifetimes to honor them with the title of doctor.

Everyone that I have met does have a medical doctor, one who works with him or her when guiding assistance is needed when health questions come up. When seeking out a physical doctor who will help them with their own special needed assistance of medical care. Each of us has the ability to "feel" an area of our body that needs attention. Through meditation, we can communicate with our doctor guide in order to receive information regarding what may be wrong with our body, what course of action to take when we develop a condition, and which physical doctor we need to see for the condition. The information you receive can vary from starting to exercise, to changing your diet, checking your medications; seek spiritual counseling, or seeking out physical medical doctor. My Doctor Guides assist me with my healthcare all the way up to the visionary messages I receive and relay to the recipient.

The Master Teacher

This is a very special guide to me for all the work I have always done. The Master Teacher imparts to us spiritual wisdom and philosophy, frequently that of the Far East appearance. Your Master Teacher may appear as Asian, Hindu, a Buddhist monk, or someone representative of India, I have even had a Moroccan Master Teacher. For a person studying a spiritual path, this guide is of great importance, and one that is overlooked or one that someone will become fixated with as his or her one and only guide. In addition, there are individuals who think if you do not know your Master Teacher then you don't know your guides. Well, I am here to say that simply is not true. We work with and know our guides when we need to and as we work more and more with them, we get to know them better. As you work in some capacity within the spiritual or metaphysical world, the guidance you receive from the Master Teacher will help you to acquire a more spiritual awareness and discernment of life in general. People who are associated with a mission for humanity and animals, or other humanitarian causes certainly are strongly influenced by their Master Teachers in all they do. The Master Teacher seems to come in around highly religious people or the disciple who fights for a worthy cause, one that is never alone in all of the work they are here to do.

Crystal Temple of the Heart

Now, you are set and ready to go onto the next level in your work as I introduce for all those who love their Crystals in **"Crystal Temple of the Heart"** where I guide you through meeting the Keeper of the Crystal and the Crystal Healing Temple.

In the Keeper of the Crystal, this is the most awesome way for you to meet the Keeper inside each crystal you have that is with you. As you journey into the heart of the crystal to meet and see whom the keeper is and why you both have chosen each other to work with, what your crystal keeper looks like and so much more to experience. This is a true experience, walking through the elements of the crystal. I love doing this meditation with my students in each new class I start.

On to journeying through the realms and entering the Crystal Temple of Healing where once the Archangel Raphael will be joining you to assist you in the healing that you need as he works with you to remove that which you are still holding onto, to taking your healing to a higher level of cleansing. Giving all to Archangel Raphael and the healing angels of Love.

Knowing Thy Self as One

Our next journey **"Knowing Thy Self as One"** of Meditation CDs will be one that I wanted to personally do as I find that most people have learned so many forms of meditation and this meditation is one that teaches not just to meditate but how to raise your vibrations the same way I do as a Visionary and Medium. One that brings your level of vibration higher to work with those in the spiritual realms in a whole new light.

It teaches you how to become more aware of those in the spiritual realms, which energy vibrations are around you and how to identify them wherever you are. Knowing thyself in all ways is what is needed as you open yourself up to more and more different energies around you. These are the exact teaching I do in my classes and I wanted to offer them to you in this unique way.

Awaken Child of One

"Awaken Child of One" is the next level of learning, as you go home to Lemuria and Atlantis, this only one of its kind Meditation takes you back to the time of your first knowing as a spiritual being. Taking you as you journey through the times from the first incarnation of who you are in Lemuria to that of who you then became to be in Atlantis. I was so excited to do this CD, as with all of them, this is one that my guides took me on to see who I really was. You know when you have those questions who am I? Well, yes, you do always get what you asked for, and I did, so I say to you what would you do if you knew who you really are? Moreover, what would you then do with it? I too had to answer those questions from my guides and teachers and when I answered it I knew I could no longer just sit and be what others wanted me to be, I had to step out and into being ME!

Egyptian Hall of Records

Welcome as we travel along to **"Egyptian Hall of Records"** there is so much talk on the Akashic Records and what really lies beneath the Sphinx. I have journeyed to the Sphinx many times in this lifetime and ones from the past and I am going to guide you in this Meditation CD. As you will be traveling beneath the Sphinx to see all that lie in wait for you to discover, whom you are to meet and then being granted admission into the right of entry of your own Akashic Records. This is an awesome journey and one you will not soon forget.

Masters Initiation of Ascension

As I bring you up in your ascension of knowing I introduce to you the **"Masters Initiation of Ascension"** this Meditation CD will guide you through the Ascended Masters initiation of ascension like nothing you have seen before. As I walk with you through the halls of the Masters, you the initiate will go through a series of acclimation levels to the grand masters arena. Enjoy!

Walking with the Blessed Mother

Nothing would be of who I am if I do not introduce you to walking with the Blessed Mother in **"Walking with the Blessed Mother."** This lovely gentle guided meditation will bring you to the place where Mother will be waiting to connect you to the pure love and compassion that only she can give to those who are ready to receive. This one will bring you to the completion of what you have always been looking for in this journey of life.

Your Journey with Jeshua

What more can I say, in **"Your Journey with Jeshua"** is an astonishing journey as I guide you back to the time when you were with Jeshua at the time of his crucifixion. One that you will know who you were in that lifetime and the love he had for you. Simply miraculous as he stands before you and speaks the words to you for you to understand what this journey of crucifixion is all about and you will know when you have completed your journey with him who you truly are from the beginning of time. The most remarkable journey in history.

Balancing the Child Within

You know I added this one of your inner child and healing within as an extra piece of what we need to understand about ourselves. In **"Balancing the Child Within"** The inner child is that of who you truly are, but are afraid to let speak. The one you keep hidden from view for you might be persecuted once again in this lifetime. Learning then the balancing of healing that which is within. Simply lovely and precious for all learning levels, whether you believe you are advanced or know you are just a newbie to everything that is here for you to behold. Beautiful!

Author Biography

Adele Linsalata - is a Internationally known Visionary Messenger, Metaphysical Teacher, Recording Artist with multiple CDs and as a gifted Clairvoyant Medium works with what is known as a sixth sense, working in the Spiritual Realms. From the age of four, spirit opened the doors for her to embrace her mission here on Mother Earth. The Blessed Mother Mary appeared to Adele and said her mission is to bridge the time and space of empowerment and unfoldment with the Children of the Light in this time of advance spiritual movement of balancing the divine feminine and masculine energy within, in order to help every person to improve their quality of life and awaken their highest potential within. Adele's teachings come as we proceed to move rapidly into a force of energy that is designed to enlighten and move the individual forward in the light to their own ascension.

As the founder of Angelic Wise Ones, Adele will teach you the tools and techniques to awaken you as you travel your spiritual journey and the ongoing reality of the spiritual realms of communications in your life. To guide and teach you as the Blessed Mother is stepping forward at this time for each of us, to connect with her energies of Divine Love, which is available to you each and every day in all you do. Bringing you to profound awareness of the divine love, wisdom and peace within you. Accessing the information, that will transform and benefit your whole life. Are you ready to be empowered to make conscious life decisions and live in total alignment with your soul's purpose every day? These courses are designed to bring you to that fulfillment as you learn from the basic foundation up to your ascension.

Adele lives and teaches in Ellicott City, Maryland with her loving husband and children who are a constant presence in her life as she lives what she teaches. Visit Adele's website at www.angelicwiseones.com.

Printed in the United States
131370LV00004B/3/P